Pathways to God

Pathways to God

An Exploration into Our Experience of God and
How We Might Grow Closer to the Divine

THOMAS EVANS

WIPF & STOCK · Eugene, Oregon

PATHWAYS TO GOD
An Exploration into Our Experience of God and How We Might Grow Closer to the Divine

Copyright © 2020 Thomas Evans. All rights reserved. Except for brief quotations in critical publications or reviews, no part of this book may be reproduced in any manner without prior written permission from the publisher. Write: Permissions, Wipf and Stock Publishers, 199 W. 8th Ave., Suite 3, Eugene, OR 97401.

All biblical quotes are drawn from the NRSV.

Wipf & Stock
An Imprint of Wipf and Stock Publishers
199 W. 8th Ave., Suite 3
Eugene, OR 97401

www.wipfandstock.com

PAPERBACK ISBN: 978-1-7252-7244-6
HARDCOVER ISBN: 978-1-7252-7245-3
EBOOK ISBN: 978-1-7252-7246-0

Manufactured in the U.S.A.   07/01/20

This book is dedicated to all those people who made it possible:

Dr. Jack R. Gallagher, who gave so much of his time and expertise.

People from a dozen congregations and on the train, who gave of their time to participate in the focus groups by sharing generously their very intimate experience of God in their lives.

Members of my congregation who participated in the survey and who so generously gave me the time and resources to conduct this project.

My parents, Bob and Abigail, who reared me in the faith and taught me the glory of faith, the gift of the mind, and the connecting power of story.

Contents

Acknowledgments		IX
1	A Journey to Discover How We Can Grow Our Experience of God	1
2	The Ways in Which We Experience God	4
3	The Survey: Measuring Our Experience of God	54
4	Going Deeper into the Data: What Drives Our Experience of God	59
5	A Practical Path to Experiencing God in Your Life	66
6	Experiencing God in Your Life through Praying the Scriptures	80
7	Experiencing God through Worship	101
8	Key Themes for Congregations	124
9	Conclusions	135
Appendix A: The Survey		143
Appendix B: The Analysis		155
Bibliography		171

Acknowledgments

Jack Ray Gallagher, EdD, MSc, Chief Scientist and Founder, Clarity Pharma Research, LLC., Spartanburg, SC, USA. Jack was an invaluable resource in the entire process of this project. He helped shape the idea and refine the methodology. Most importantly he provided his considerable expertise through his analysis of the data.

The Survey Analysis in Appendix B is entirely his work.

1

A Journey to Discover How We Can Grow Our Experience of God

Our hearts are restless, until they can find rest in you.
St. Augustine of Hippo[1]

AUGUSTINE'S FAMOUS QUOTE GREW from an age of violence, power, and greed and his own personal pursuits of sex, gluttony, and the horror of the Coliseum. He increasingly finds this life unfulfilling, empty, and perverse and through Scripture discovers the true fulfillment of his quest: a life filled with the wonder and glory of God.

Throughout my twenty-five years as a minister, I have constantly battled with the feeling that church somehow falls well short of what it could be, that we have failed by and large to connect the majority of our people to the powerful presence of our Lord with Augustine—like enthusiasm. My tradition is Presbyterian, specifically the PCUSA.

Both my parents are Presbyterian ministers and since I was a boy, I have been a part of this denomination. I am filled with deep admiration and thanksgiving for how we approach Christianity, but also a profound frustration with our sometimes myopic perspectives that lead to a perverse pride in how we approach the faith.

My father is progressive, and my mother is conservative, and through my years I have learned to deeply appreciate both perspectives. I have found myself agreeing with the progressive social stances of the denomination

---

1. Augustine, *Confessions*, 1.1.1.

while at the same time filled with the conservative's longing for a denomination more deeply connected to prayer, Scripture, and surrender to God—in short, a denomination more in love with God and people than with procedures, politics, and polity.

I have come to the conclusion that the Presbyterian church, like many individuals and institutions, suffers perhaps most greatly from its strengths. We were born in an age of excess and abuse of power, and our inherent mistrust of emotional approaches and our focus on the intellect allowed us to shape a church that profoundly impacted history and helped us, along with the rest of the Reformation, to reshape not only the church but the world.

But these strengths, these tactics, have led us away from the most central aspect of the faith: the power and presence of God and a life wholly given over to our Lord Jesus. Without knowing it, we have replaced God with procedure and votes, thinking somehow majority rule automatically creates the will of God. We have forgotten how to be people of prayer and piety, and we have forgotten most of all the distinction between the power of the church through its people and the power of God.

We have forgotten that the only true possibility for change is God dwelling richly in the hearts of women and men. In the days of the Hebrew Scriptures we see time and again the failure of the external laws to forge Israel into the people God wanted them to be. We heard the call of the prophets for a time when God's laws would be written not on stone, but on people's hearts.

I have regularly attended and served Presbyterian churches in thirteen states, in places as diverse as rural Arkansas and the hive of Manhattan. I have found these churches filled with faithful people who love God and others and want their congregation to be as faithful and vibrant as the Lord would allow.

At the same time, I have sensed a defeatism present in the DNA of many congregations, and it stems I think from the realization that their friends and neighbors generally opt out of church, and even the ones that do attend do so less and less.

There are various theories as to why football stadiums and concert venues explode with people and the churches do not.

But the axiom under which I operate is nothing can possibly be more compelling than the power and presence of God! And if we can find a way authentic to our tradition to tap into this presence, then our attendance challenges would be a thing of the past. But that of course is not our goal.

As in the days of Augustine, we live in times of violence and greed. Today the level of mistrust of one another is like a toxin in the water supply—no one wants to dip their cup in fellowship with others for fear we will be poisoned. News outlets are reaping billions sowing these seeds of fear and mistrust, but the church has failed to raise its voice that there is another way. People in this country are feeling more and more soul-sick like Augustine, and we need to find a way to connect them to the source of all life.

However, our history has made us wary of manipulating people's emotions simply to fill the pews and rightly so.

But as an executive presbyter, I saw the tragedy of not finding our way as a church as dozens of congregations closed their doors and the last members turned out the lights.

This tragedy is a result of our amnesia. We have forgotten how to convey the wonder of the majesty and mystery of God, and the churches became milquetoast and, dare we say, boring.

Other Christian traditions have always had unique ways to experience God. In December of 2018, I attended an Episcopalian service at the Princeton University chapel. It was Lessons and Carols and, before it was over, I felt like I had been ushered into the throne room of heaven.

I have listened to the readings, smelled the incense, and heard choirs and brass many times before. But on this day it came together in such a way that by the end when the procession walked out of the church, I watched them all the way down the aisle, wanting to see the crucifer until she walked out the door because something in that service touched my soul deeply, beyond intellect or reason and beyond human control and contrivance.

After this service I reflected on the ways other traditions cultivate an experience of the divine in worship. The Baptists have their altar calls and testimonies, the Catholics venerate the host, the Orthodox kiss their icons, and the Evangelicals raise their hands and are slain in the Spirit.

But since God is divine and active everywhere, I knew that God was and is powerfully and profoundly present in Presbyterian churches, too. In every congregation I have been a part of as a pastor or parishioner, I have known the love of God through that place. I have known people who have life-changing experiences in our churches that have knocked them flat.

And so, I set out on a quest. I wanted to know what churches can do to cultivate the experience of God in the lives of their congregants and those beyond their walls. And too, since I knew that God was already at work in people's lives in these churches, I decided to conduct twelve focus groups in congregations from South Carolina to New York to California. And for good measure I took the train across the country and decided to learn from fellow passengers as well.

2

The Ways in Which We Experience God

IN THE FOCUS GROUPS and random conversations on the train, I listened to the ways in which the church was connecting people to God and the stumbling blocks we sometimes place before them. I also learned, at least anecdotally, which factors cultivate these experiences and which factors militate against them.

Fundamental to the human experience is the need to find union with God. I believe learning better how to do this will of course benefit the individuals whom we touch, but that it will also benefit our churches and society. Because without the presence of God in our lives, not only are our hearts restless, but they are broken as well. And this brokenness manifests itself in all the worst ways humans can imagine.

The participants in these focus groups offered tremendous insight, not so much in the uniqueness of the information (I suspect you won't be surprised at very much of it), but by the nuances of their stories from which we can learn.

I began most of the sessions with a brief questionnaire that sought to glean some insight as a basis for conversation. The preliminary quantitative data was not so much surprising as it was disheartening. People barely experienced God more in worship than in their daily life. They encountered God more often in mission than in worship and most frequently in nature.

I realize that according to our Presbyterian understanding, worship is our service to God, that it is for God's glory and not our own benefit. And even though I agree with that, somehow this explanation seems insufficient.

We are missing part of the story, for it is clear in Scripture that God was known powerfully in worship.

Over 95 percent experienced God when they least expected it, speaking to the vitality of the Holy Spirit in the world today.

The universal response, no matter how much they were currently experiencing God in their life, was that everyone wanted more God, from the most ardent lover of God to the most casual detached participant. So not only was Augustine right about our hearts being restless, but in this life, we will never fully be at rest in the Lord's loving arms, so we are always left hungering for more. What else could we possibly need to motivate our congregations to change than people's palpable hunger for God?

Of course, this desire for more God left me wondering. If everyone wants more God, what is it that they really want? What do they mean by this?

As I conducted the focus groups, it became clear what was in their hearts. People yearn for more mystery in their life—not the kind you find in a cheap dime-store novel, but the mystery shaded by awe and delight in that which is beyond comprehension. They don't want the domesticated Jesus we are tempted to peddle in our churches. They don't want "Buddy Christ" and they most certainly don't want our God to be like the father from *Leave It to Beaver*! They want to know better the God of creation and chaos, the God of eternity who has the power to create the world and everything in it!

People want deeper connections forged by the Spirit and more hope in a world that increasingly feels fractured and filled with daily despair. People want more purpose and more peace. They ache for a greater sense of belonging and to be healed spiritually as well as physically.

They want to be loved and feel love; they yearn to feel love for others; they ache for it. They want to feel their empathy stretched, growing their love for all types of people. But the world works terribly hard against this. God made us to love one another; people have it within them, but the world tamps it down by teaching us to fear others by leading us to believe "they" are robbing us of our rights and our future. People want more God so they can leave behind narcissism and perfectionism and have hearts fully open to the abuse, racism, and poverty that so many in this world carry. People desperately want us to open that love in them.

People want to feel the life of the Spirit's breath bringing them strength during what is at times profound weariness from the trials of life. People want more God within them so that their faith can grow bigger and stronger, enabling them to live a life of great courage and risk. They want to grow into God, into all that God made them to be.

People want that courage of God in their hearts so they can be more fully themselves, living a life of greater authenticity and deeper vulnerability.

And so, as I listened to this longing, in the midst of these interviews I realized this project is a very personal one for me as well. Certainly, as a pastor I want to know better how to serve my congregation; yes, I want to be able to connect my members to God more effectively, but I too want to experience more God in my life.

I am at a time of transition in my life. The purpose that drove me for the last thirty years has changed. My glorious children have moved out of the house and are forging their own lives now. Wendy and I have the gift of more time together, but we have yet to figure out how to spend this much quality time without driving each other crazy! I learned she really does not need (or want!) my views on upholstery material.

Suddenly I am fixated with, of all things—shoes, something I never cared or paid attention to before. I have come to love the feel of quality leather and to admire excellent craftsmanship. I have learned about the quality of Goodyear welted shoes vs. cemented ones. I know that "last" is the word for the shape of the shoe, and I know Northampton is the place quality English shoes are made. Why do I know all of this? Why do I care?

I realize that I am filling my life up with more "things" when what my soul really yearns for is more God.

I want to know more deeply the depth of that love God has for me; I want to quench that hunger in my spirit, and I want to know how to live God's purpose in my life as a father, husband, pastor, friend. This is the life God has given me, and I want it to be overflowing in my soul with what I know in my head to be true.

And as I think about these focus groups, one thing is profoundly clear. And it is good news! Despite the problems in our congregations and the challenges we face, I left each one of these sessions in awe and gratitude. The God of Abraham and Sarah, of Isaac and Rebekah, of Jacob and . . . is a God powerfully and wonderfully at work in the lives of those in our pews.

I found that people experience God:

- through others,
- through nature,
- through the arts,
- through study,
- through "prayer,"
- through acts of service,
- through acts of love/kindness,
- through anything, any anytime, anywhere.

As I surveyed these experiences, they grouped into at least seven different categories. This set of seven can help us all better know the various places in which we might help people connect more powerfully and regularly to the presence of God: Holy Presence, Holy Communion, Holy Revelation, Holy Purpose, Holy Power and Providence, Holy Grace, and Holy Love.

HOLY PRESENCE: AN ECSTATIC, AWE-FILLED SURGE OF THE POWERFUL, MYSTERIOUS PRESENCE OF GOD

"Come no closer! Remove the sandals from your feet, for the place on which you are standing is holy ground."

Exodus 3:5

When Moses ventured toward the bush that burned with fire but was not consumed, he experienced the Holy Presence of God. He heard the Lord tell him as much when God commanded him to take his shoes off, "for he was standing on holy ground." As I listened to people share their stories, "Holy Presence" captured a collection of experiences from listening to a joyful piece of music in worship to a 9/11 memorial service.

One person described these experience as "being outside of myself." It was while witnessing an act of kindness. It was not so much a moment of admiration that we often have, but it was a jolt of holy joy and a disembodiment in which her soul was wrapped in the presence of God. She was literally gasping for breath. These moments knock you flat because, well, because it's pure, godly presence!

By and large, Presbyterians do little to cultivate a worship that is filled with mystery and awe. Whereas the Catholics have the Veneration of the Host (praying before consecrated communion bread because they literally believe Jesus is in that bread), we have largely replaced a God of mystery, power, and wonder with a God known through voting, procedures, and carefully planned liturgy that does not try to expect something as surprising as God showing up in worship!

Now, the Orthodox not only kiss their icons, but there is screen that only the priest can go behind, suggesting that God is amazingly, powerfully, and even dangerously present in worship. At one Orthodox service I attended, I was told there was an actual piece of the cross of Christ placed there.

My twenty-first-century brain scoffed at the idea. In fact, I had to suppress a laugh I was so caught off guard by this incredulous information. But that evening, in between sleep and wakefulness, I saw a vision of the priest coming out from behind that screen glowing just as Moses did after spending time in the presence of God! It was (W)Hol(l)y Unexpected!

There are at least two exceptions within Presbyterian traditions: Christmas Eve candlelight services and Maundy Thursday services. The candlelight services deliberately dim the lights to create a frame of wonder as we anticipate the birth of Christ. It is serene joy. But not all moments of Holy Presence are happy.

One participant talked about experiencing God's presence most powerfully during the "long, sad Maundy Thursday service." It was a combination of the Scriptures revealing the most agonizing moment in history with the gradual extinguishing of the light. Despite the deep sorrow, several participants shared that this was their favorite service of the year.

How Our Worship Can Cultivate Holy Presence

The challenge here stems from our mistrust of what we might perceive as manipulation or manufactured experiences. One focus group participant described his experience at a Christian camp.

> I have only had one dramatic tearful experience and it was at camp: it was orchestrated, but it worked for me. . . . all these crazy athletes bawling . . . three or four days later I realized I would never go back to that, but it did not displace the strong feeling . . . but it is counterproductive; to expect that kind of moment . . .

As a result of these experiences and our theological misgivings with other traditions' practices, we have failed to find our own unique way. However, our worship services might do more with the interplay of light and text to cultivate these moments. We can choose music that tells of God's majesty through the words and the arrangement. The organist can choose registrations that underscore this aspect of God, and the liturgy can tell of God's actions throughout history.

The preacher can check his or her ego at the door and be willing to ascribe certain texts and divine actions to that which is beyond us in understanding and power rather than trying to explain away any paradoxes within an infinitely powerful God.

We Presbyterians love to understand, but one former medical doctor pointed out the distinction between explaining and exploring.

> I no longer try to turn it into a completely explained rational phenomenon . . . I wanted everything explained as a medical student, but the further I went along . . . the mystery came back in; science does not explain everything. . . . The further I got down the path of faith, the less important explaining it all seemed to be; I am happy with mystery but want to keep exploring it.

Another person discovered the pastor helped her experience God through creating a sense of expectation. It came in the pastor's opening invitation to worship.

> You might be here for your own reasons but be ready. God has you here for his reasons, and God is in control of this time we have together, and God is going to do something in your life right now.

She found his welcome developed a sense of expectation in worship. Of course, we pastors often shy away from such bold statements. We know someone will come to us telling us nothing happened, no bright lights, or tingling of the spine. We shy away because we fear being exposed as a fraud. But it is time to put away the fear and be bold in the name of Christ

The Power of Nature to Connect Us to God's Presence

With so many people from the focus groups citing nature as a key place of connection to the divine, I wanted to better understand precisely what is in nature the enables these experiences. I spent much of my childhood exploring national parks but never made it to the Southwest, so I decided to head to the Grand Canyon and Zion National Park.

And just between you and me I used no deodorant for a month. The dry heat really does make a difference!

I wanted to set out on two of the most iconic hikes in the Southwest, if not in the world. The first was the Bright Angel Trail in the Grand Canyon. I hiked this one in solitude trying to emulate the ancient practice of the desert fathers so that in facing nature alone I might discover something about myself. The second, the Narrows Top-Down trail in Zion National Park, I would hike with my daughter, Liz.

I had not done any serious backpacking for thirty years and as you will hear I didn't really know what I was doing. The night before I set out in the canyon I went shopping and I began to worry if I would have enough food, so I wound up buying twelve pounds' worth, including three pounds of candy for three nights! My pack weighed over forty pounds and I had failed to train with that much weight. Critical error number one!

Of course, the scenery was everything I hoped, and I was filled with positive energy as I began at five in the morning to descend nine miles down a rock trail with a 4500-foot drop in elevation. Critical error number two! My friend and Grand Canyon expert, Tom King, had advised me to depart at 4:00 a.m. but I didn't think it would make much of a difference! Tom, I will be sure to listen next time! Because I left too late, I wound up carrying that pack in 110-degree heat!

By the time I arrived at the campsite my calves, my thighs, my knees, my ankles, and even my toes were absolutely shot! I threw off my pack and simply sat in the creek for about thirty minutes to cool off.

I spent the next twelve hours recovering from heat exhaustion, moving from the creek to cool off to my tent to rest. I was utterly spent.

The next day I had gained some strength back and finally had a chance to enjoy the beauty of nature. I even figured out how to make my pillow comfortable so I could rest easily and begin to see the wonders around me,

> tenacious squirrels seeking out crumbs,
> insects swirling about looking for scraps of food,
> birds of prey soaring across the stark incredibly blue sky,
> all with the backdrop of the insanely beautiful rock formations of THE canyon.

The colors were so incredibly rich, and combined with the reality that it all took millions of years to form it was almost too much for my mind to comprehend. It was everything I had hoped for. I could not imagine something this inspiring and powerful existed in all the world.

However, it began to dawn on me that I would have to carry myself back up those nine miles of trail uphill this time, with forty pounds of torture on my back.

I absolutely dreaded the thought, so I kept trying to think of a way to lighten my backpack. I considered leaving some food behind or some supplies, but the park had signs everywhere commanding us to take out everything!

Even the garbage cans had signs not to throw anything in them!

I had decided to take this trip to see what it was like relying on my on my own strength and my very limited knowledge of backpacking and as I sought rest, I encountered an internal struggle and paradoxical thoughts.

My mind was racing both with the joy of experiencing the canyon and the pain of self-doubt, truly wondering if I could make it back up.

And so, while at the bottom of *the* canyon as the temperature topped 120, in my overheated delirium, I began to reflect on our connection to creation.

And I realized it is the difference between dipping and diving.

Nature is something people have a strong attachment to, and millions love going to the beach each year, as do I,

> but not if the sun is too hot
> or the water is too cold
> or the sand is too sandy.

I am more likely to dip my toes in the water than to dive in these days.

Most prefer a mere dip of nature, and it was quite clear at the canyon that this was the case. According to one Grand Canyon website something like 90 percent of the people never make it out of the Grand Canyon Village to go below the rim.

I certainly love being comfortable, and I don't think I could live in the South if it wasn't air conditioned. But occasionally we need to fully immerse ourselves in nature to remind ourselves once again of where we come from and who we are in relation to this world and the God who created it.

The heat prostration and the pain at first reminded me of the expulsion from the garden of Eden in Genesis 3. I thought once again about my sore legs, and the journey back up the canyon and I was reminded that I was on the other side of paradise,

> the side to which we have been expelled,
> in which the ground only brings forth toil,
> and in which the animals of the earth would bite our heal and bruise our souls.

It reminded me there is something fundamentally out of balance with the world and perhaps more than we know, the problems of our world stem from this disconnection.

As the sun continued to heat up, I realized these cynical thoughts might be the result of an overheated brain! So, I decided to immerse myself once again in the creek, to cool my head and refresh my spirit. And it worked! The cynical thoughts quickly turned, as I realized that despite the toil we are still drawn to creation.

Because in nature we encounter something that is God's domain and it is absolutely and utterly beyond us, beyond our capabilities, while at the same time its power, its color, its ancientness draws us to it.

Genesis teaches us we were forged amid nature and placed in Eden, that is paradise, and in perfect harmonic balance with everything. And so, we are pulled into nature, because deep within our created consciousness we yearn, we ache sometimes painfully so to return to this idyllic state, to return to the garden.

We don't simply have a love for nature. We are nature and we want to be a part of it, as we were meant to be, once again.

And as a cool breeze wafted through the canyon (a little gift from above) I looked at those canyon rock formations and colors shaped by water, pressure, and time and I saw them as the very brushstrokes of God! Not metaphorically but truly. When you are out there you can see it, you can feel the presence of God standing right there looking over her handiwork! The presence was so very real! So palpable. As real as the air we take into our lungs... every breath!

To be in the midst of it all... was to become a part of a wonderful and complex symphony... the melody and the meaning of which I can't quite understand. Its beauty was so piercing and powerful, so complex and rich. At moments it was too much to behold and I had to look away. I realized this desire to commune with nature is a primal and unthought desire to return to paradise, to a place of perfect harmony with our God. This is why pain and sickness and heat, sweat, and toil do more than physically debilitate us; they remind us of the schism in which we all live. I believe it is these factors that led so many to speak of nature as a powerful place of connection to God.

HOLY COMMUNION: AN EXPERIENCE OF SACRED, DEEP CONNECTION AND A SENSE OF PROFOUND UNITY WITH OTHERS ON A LEVEL BEYOND KINSHIP OR FRIENDSHIP

All of you are one in Christ Jesus.

GALATIANS 3:28B

When the apostle Paul spoke of the church, he thought of it more as a living, breathing body because of how intricately God weaves us with our brothers and sisters in Christ. As he wrote, "All are one in Christ."

People spoke of a moment on a mission trip that, while holding hands after a long day's work, knit them into a unified whole. Being together far away from home, for a shared purpose, embedded a sense of kinship with others they barely knew. These were people not prone to holding hands in church or when they prayed under "normal conditions." But for some reason, it was the most natural thing in the world to grasp that hand next to them during that week together, even if the men couldn't resist a giggle.

Someone else experienced Holy Communion at the time of officer examinations saying, "We really were one." At the conclusion of officer training at this church, all the first-year people give a statement of faith. It is a moment of deep sharing.

One member explained,

> From an old Baptist boy, they are really testimonies! I have watched the whole group—by the time it is done they have become a group. You don't forget the stories and all the differences to know that they are really together from different backgrounds. It is just . . . [so powerful]. In every person you can see God is at work in their lives.

And the pastor said, "It is an ugly cry, no holding back. It is so powerful, and people ask how can we do more of this? Humor, tears, laughter is always wonderful and always profound."

It was the vulnerability and honesty within the faith statements that engendered a deep sense of respect and mutual valuing. Judgments and prejudgments of one another dissolved away as they experienced the truth of Paul's words—all are one in Christ.

For another person the experience of Holy Communion during communion by intinction "happens every time."

> Seeing her friend whose husband died,
> the father fighting addiction to alcohol,
> a five-year-old little girl,
> and a ninety-year-old with a walker
> all in the same line,
> going to the same place,
> for the same reason,
> is sheer joy and delight.
> It helps her to visually see our oneness in Christ and reassures her, in the depth of her being, that in Jesus there
> truly
> . . . is
> . . . NO
> . . . distinction!

Another moment of Holy Communion was powerful because of the reconciliation it created. A church had gone through dramatic conflict and as a result several members were at odds with one another.

One person said,

> A man who thought I was lying and myself became known as being at odds. On one "High Holy Sunday" we were going to process, and someone was missing. I counted the people and I saw that we were going to line up together and march down the aisle next to each other before the entire congregation . . . and I got nervous . . . but I felt like it was the presence of God to remind us we were part of the same body.

Clearly this event was not orchestrated, but the Spirit will work where it will. But other people noticed what was happening. She continued, "The pastor came to me and said, 'I saw who you were walking in with and I noticed.' Then the next Sunday the guy came up to me and gave me a gift. He felt the same."

God made us to be in union with others and, when that is broken, it leaves a hole in our heart. When we can find ways to bring reconciliation, the power will be palpable.

Many have had this experience of holy unity beyond a gathering of just Christians. Moments of historic tragedy that bring the community together have powerfully evoked this experience. After 9/11, someone described a community service with Jews, Muslims, Christians, and agnostics in which everyone gathered in the same place for the same purpose, with the same needs and the same hopes. For this person, it was as if the Holy Spirit had woven a thread of hope through each person's heart, connecting them all.

Others, especially in churches filled with visible diversity, found this connection during the passing of the peace. In one New York church with African Americans, Anglos, and Hispanics, and also people of economic, gender, and sexuality diversity, seeing them all milling about during that moment of holy greeting was a visible sign of hope and of the kingdom of God as the Lord intends it. It gave one couple such hope and peace that they committed to joining that church the first Sunday they visited.

When you consider Holy Communion as a "oneness" with God's creation, many experienced it most deeply in nature. This was distinct from the stories of knowing God's presence in nature. Whether it was watching birds at a feeder or walking through the Redwoods, the serene peace of God's handiwork shed their hyper-sense of individuality and made them truly feel a part of the whole—the whole of God's creation.

How Might the Church Foster the Experience of Holy Communion?

In some churches, the passing of the peace is fraught with friction. Some feel like it is an interruption to a service of reverence and there are moments when I have felt that as well. Those who objected to it in the focus groups were willing to go along when they received a better understanding of its purpose and its roots.

The same couple so enamored with the practice in their new church resisted it in their former church because they felt its doctrine, along with its lack of diversity, militated against the very purpose of the passing of the peace. The need for the church to be authentic in its practices played a critical role in how people experienced God.

When the passing of the peace works well, it seems to have a deep impact. A man in one focus group said, "We can go deeper; we don't just connect on Sunday, Passing the Peace takes a long time . . ." (He was right! I worshiped with them that Sunday and for a moment I thought the service had concluded!) And as the man finished a woman added, "The difference with other friends and church friends is you may be the only Christ anyone sees today." So, in ways we don't realize, in those few moments of shaking hands, even when people aren't saying, "The peace of Christ be with you," some are thinking holy thoughts and becoming spiritual sustenance to help others through the week.

It was also very telling to discover how powerful and meaningful holding hands during prayer was on mission trips and special meetings. People yearn for physical connection to one another, but our defenses and fears have made this problematic in many situations. I think a carefully earnest cultivation of physical contact with others, especially during moments of worship, can greatly increase the frequency and power of Holy Communion.

One person described people as "Icebergs," borrowing from Eric Law's writings. We mostly only see about a third of the person, while the rest is below the surface. Like icebergs, it is what is below the surface that sinks us when we ram into each other.

The moments of sharing statements of faith in church board meetings worked to create deep community because it gave everyone a chance to share from the heart and value each person's story and contribution to the whole. So, a church must carefully cultivate this shared sense of togetherness through an astute understanding of the various people who are present.

Curiously, almost no focus group had anything to say about experiencing God during the Lord's Supper, except for the example cited earlier. In fact, when I specifically asked people if they experienced God through communion, they would nod their heads but never elaborate. I think there is profound opportunity to make changes to the Lord's Supper as a means of connecting people to the presence of God. I suspect this lack of communion stories would not have existed in focus groups from Catholic congregations.

My Experience of Holy Communion/Community in Nature

The text which illuminates this experience, "All are one in Christ," may be short but it says it all. This is all the verse we need because it says it all with no qualifications, provisos, or exceptions.

The oneness is absolute.

Through the power of Christ's love, we are powerfully, wonderfully, joyfully, and unequivocally fused to everyone.

I discovered the depth of this Holy Communion, of this oneness with nature, God, and others during a trip out west. After my Grand Canyon trip in solitude I then went to Zion National Park with my daughter, Liz.

We decided on the Top-Down Narrows hike, a sixteen-mile trek through the Virgin River. Some who have been on it described as their favorite hike in the world! And I must agree.

The preparation for the trip was complex since we were doing a through hike. It took us at least ten hours of research simply to decide on footwear! Even so, by the end, our ankles, toes, and shins were shredded and bruised from thousands of awkward steps on endless boulders. Despite its complexity, it was a much smoother hike than the Grand Canyon because instead of relying on my own ineptitude, my daughter, Liz, coordinated the details. Even my backpack was lighter since I had less food to carry and I was able to leave excess clothing in our rental car.

We took a van with six others to our drop off point. The hike began in a wide meadow with mountains in the distance. The river started off more like a creek—about six feet wide. We hoisted our packs and pulled out our trekking poles. These were invaluable in finding footholds on the rocks, while preventing the river from sweeping us away. At the start it was thigh deep, but the depth of the river varied from as low as our ankles to over our heads. Perhaps the most fun we had were the few times we had to swim in the icy river with our packs on our backs.

As the minutes turned to hours, the green fields and low riverbank transformed into variegated rock wall hundreds of feet high. In some ways, it was the opposite of the Grand Canyon, trading off the incredible expanse of the Grand Canyon with the enclosed, narrow, thirty-foot shoot of the

Virgin River and trading off my time of solitude to be with Liz. This truly was a once in a lifetime event.

On one level, there was simply spending time together away from the distractions of civilization, but I also believe God was doing something more profound. As I looked on those sheer rock walls, I felt that same harmony and glory of creation that I did in the canyon. Liz was also there having the same awe-filled experience. But a third thing was happening as well. There was something electric about sharing this surreal and beautiful setting with her.

The bonds of love and harmony with Liz were magnified by this profound moment of Holy Community amid God's creation! And it showed me Liz in another way. Not only as my daughter, but as God's child, driven, and able to teach me so much. I saw her as her own person, a strong young woman, capable and able to conquer any quest she set her mind to. Even one that Dad would never want her to do!

And at least in part her power was driven by the strength of Holy Community with other people found in the parks. For Holy Community not only enhances our sense of kinship with others but it can give us strength to conquer great challenges in life.

For me, the Narrows hike was all the challenge I needed in Zion and it met all my expectations. But there is another world-class hike there, called Angel's Landing, and even thinking about it terrifies me. It is called that because only angels would dare go to the top. The first two miles are a rather straightforward hike up a beautiful mountain. It is a well-paved trail, safe, inviting, and pleasant.

> The last half mile is all done on a narrow cliff
> ... sometimes only a few feet wide,
> ... with one-thousand-foot drops on either side!

It takes over an hour and half to do this section because there are hundreds of people scrambling up the rock, most of whom are trying to hold on for dear life to the single chain that poses as a safety measure on the climb. For anyone afraid of heights this multiplies the terror because you may wind up standing in one place for minutes with only the sheer drop to think about.

Liz had wanted to do the hike, but I thought I had convinced her that we were too tired from the Narrows. But that is when God put the Holy Community to work.

In the day after the Narrows hike, we decided to take a tour bus to see more of the park. While on that bus we heard one person declare, "Angel's landing will be the best hike you ever do in your life!" This piqued Liz's interest. A few minutes later while enjoying a cup of coffee at Zion Lodge, a man who just came from Angel's landing told us, "I have done it five times. I would not trade that experience for the world!" The final nail in the coffin, so to speak, happened when we ran into a couple we previously met on the Narrows, who said, "Absolutely do it! You will want to turn back, but don't. It is fantastic!"

Well I wasn't going to do this hike, but clearly this Holy Community of hikers had inspired Liz so off we went. I stopped after the first two miles, but Liz went on the narrow cliff to head for the top. Immediately, my heart dropped into my throat. And my mind kept racing through the worst scenario that would come from one errant step.

After about forty-five minutes I began to wonder if something had happened to her. I thought certainly she would have returned by now.

People kept coming off the mountain, some terrified others nonplussed. One family said, "The Vegas strip was much more dangerous!" Another said, "You want to know what is really terrifying, the porta potty just up the hill over there!"

After an hour, I was a complete wreck.

I started asking every person who came off the hike if they had seen her. I asked them when they set off to try and determine if she should be down by now.

After an hour and a half, I was convinced something had happened.

After all, two young men said the whole thing only took them thirty minutes! (I suspect they were lying!) But then the blessing of Holy Community went to work.

A couple that had passed us on the way up just came off the climb! And as I spoke to them, they assured me that if tragedy had struck, they would have heard. Even though I was not fully convinced, their compassion and understanding offered me . . . not peace exactly . . . but a measure of comfort in my agony. Their sympathy gave me hope.

So maybe Liz was okay . . .

And then glory! A few minutes later there she was! I have never felt so relieved in my life. But even so, the terror and its aftereffects lasted deep into that night as I had horrific dreams of that hike!

I asked Liz how in the world she made the hike and she too experienced the power of Holy Community. She said,

> Cautious Confidence. You have to be careful the whole way, but at the same time believe you can make it. The confidence comes from all the encouragement on the way up. A man said to me, "You're doing a good job." Someone else said, "I want to tell you

you're almost there but you're really not. But don't give up! Keep going!"

In these simple words she found great strength and was able to continue to climb.

It happened to be Sunday and after the "hike of horrible horror" on the way down we overheard a conversation between a young girl and her father. "Dad, this is way better than being in church!"

And the dad turned to her motioning to the people and the wonder of God's creation while saying, "Honey, this IS church!"

This is what makes all the communities of faithful followers so wonderful, amazing, and powerful. Holy Community is a bond given by God for each other, given to us by Christ.

And together as those communities encounter the beauty of life in one another and in God's creation, the unity and the love enable them to give one another strength and hope for whatever we face in this life as we look forward to joy in the next.

HOLY REVELATION: AN AWAKENING TO A DEEP TRUTH WITH PROFOUND CLARITY; HOLY INSIGHT INTO GOD, LIFE, AND THE WORLD

"You will know the truth, and the truth will make you free."

JOHN 8:32

Sometimes all people need is to hear what they already know in their heart. The most inspiring sermons are rarely the most creative. They simply tell the old, old story with eyes on today's challenges. Hearing of the power of God's grace can light a person's soul with God's love.

The marker for many of the participants around a sermon that impacted them was one that led them to conversations after church.

> "They hit *home* about everyday life not just theology."
> "[The pastor] brings it down to our level."
> "There is not *one Sunday* that we don't come home and talk about what she has preached."

The sermons that people connect God's revelation to are the ones that connect their lives to the story. One person said,

> The sermons move me, too. It was a sermon last month...around the MLK holiday...the pastor talked about an experience as kid

digging with African Americans and how things have changed . . . I liked it 'cause I could identity with it.

The sermon referred to a past that the parishioner could relate to. This enabled him to find God's truth in the pastor's words.

God's word reveals unique, profound, and challenging truths that without the Bible we would never know because they are not obvious. Not only is Scripture God's unique revelation but the greatest truths are absolutely contrary to our natural instincts.

Truths like,

In the image of God, he created them . . .
(How is it possible a small, semi-hairy biped that lives for about fourscore years carries the image of the infinite and unimaginable God?)

Or, *I will forgive your evil deeds, I will remember your sins no more . . .*
(If there is one thing in the Bible we don't really believe, its this one. Other religions come to very different conclusions. God not only forgives us but forgets all those sins as well. Forgiven is forgiven and forgiven means FORGOTTEN!)

Or, *the Word was made flesh, and dwelt among us . . . full of grace and truth*
(This infinite God came down . . . shrunk down, out of love, to redeem us.)

Throughout my ministry people have shared stories of the power of God's word in their lives.

The illuminating text for this God experience, "If you continue in my word . . . You shall know the truth and the truth will set you free" (John 8:32), is once again simple, brief, and filled with life-altering possibilities.

The promise we have from embracing God's Holy Revelation comes from the Lord himself . . . freedom. Freedom from worry. Freedom from pain. Freedom from guilt. Freedom to do what is right with the courage to face whatever the consequences might be.

Freedom from Fear

Thou art with me.

PSALM 23:4

One person I encountered in my research found the recitation of the twenty-third Psalm to be especially important. It was right after a 9/11 during an interfaith service. They all said the words together, and when they came to the phrase, "Yea though I walk through the valley of the shadow of death, I will fear no evil because thou art with me," she suddenly felt deep in her soul that God was in fact with her, with all of those worshiping, and indeed the whole world. It was not new to her, not at all. Even so at that moment God revealed to her (Holy Revelation) in a powerful new way, the reality of her/his awesome, loving presence.

Freedom to Say "Yes"!

"Go from your country and your kindred..."

GENESIS 12:1

Because Holy Revelation mostly comes through Scripture one focus group emphasized the importance of teaching Scripture more thoroughly. The participants explained that knowing God's truth and understanding God's actions in biblical times set them free to see God at work in their lives and in the world today. After completing a multi-year Bible study, she said, "It made you get to know God.... You see how he worked through the ages; it opened my eyes to how he was working in my life."

Another woman agreed, saying Bible study was key to unlocking God's will for her own life. Knowing scriptural truth emboldened her to say "yes." She said,

> Bible study was key.... Take Abraham.... God, told him to just leave and go.... When the church asked for volunteers to lead the children's weekly ministry [I knew] God was wanting me to step out in faith... and I did it.

Knowing when to say "yes" to an opportunity is not easy. In fact, often we fail to live in the freedom of truth because at first it feels like an awful burden. Especially all that Jesus asks of us!

Freedom to Obey

"Walk only in the way that I command you, so that it may be well with you."

JEREMIAH 7:23

Jesus' sayings are all hard stuff... party ending stuff... boring stuff... but at one point you will see it, the light will come on, and all the hard work of living the faith daily will pay off.

You remember the movie *The Karate Kid*. Daniel spent hours in the hot sun on Saturday afternoons and after school painting Mr. Miyagi's fence, sanding his deck, and waxing his cars.

> It felt like wasted time...
> it felt like it had nothing to do with his life goals...
> it felt like it had nothing to do with learning karate!

Instead of feeling free he was sore, tired, and out of time and when his anger boiled over, the Karate Kid suddenly saw the truth, the truth that set him free, when Mr. Miyagi said, "Wax on!" "Wax off" "Paint the Fence." At that moment the truth of his training was revealed, and he was set free. He discovered that the whole time his wise master had been training him.

When we obey God's commands it can be hard at first. This is why knowing God's word is critical. It is filled with examples like Jacob who endured great hardship when he failed to trust God's ways. He stole his brother's birthright and blessing and as a result he was on the run from Esau for forty years! But when his attitude and heart changed so did his life.

Freedom to Do the Right Thing

When life shows us two diverging roads the strength to choose God's path comes from turning to God's word, but it is not always obvious.

After graduating from Princeton Seminary in the 1920s my grandfather faced a hard decision: leave the Presbyterian Church to help form a new, more orthodox denomination, or stay and try to reform. He chose to renounce the PCUSA, believing it to no longer be God's church, and for twenty years he was a leader in the Orthodox Presbyterian denomination.

Over these years he saw this new denomination split not once but twice more and he felt a growing unease about his decision.

Ironically, even though he believed the PCUSA was not obedient to God's word he realized he had not turned to Scripture to learn what he should do about it! He had not sought God's word for guidance about his decision.

After a thorough study of God's word, he was shocked by what he discovered. Time and time again God's will in times of disagreement and disobedience is to remain together! Not to leave!

And so, now he decided to be obedient to God's word which tells us, if we confess our sins, he who is faithful and just will forgive us our sins and cleanse us from all unrighteousness (1 John 1:19). It was his moment of Holy Revelation. He returned to the Presbyterian Church by standing before those he had earlier condemned, and he said, "It was wrong of me to do what I did."

His confession set him free to return to the path God had for him.

Freedom in Christ

Ultimately, Holy Revelation is not about learning the Bible. Here is why.

One Tuesday afternoon I attended a Rotary program featuring a Teddy Roosevelt impersonator. Teddy is one of those presidents that stands out in our minds as being a forceful personality who made bold decisions, some of them of lasting greatness like creating the National Parks system.

But beyond a few vague impressions and forgotten facts, that was all he was to me. An important historical figure. But the impersonator changed that. It was not simply because it was informative, though I did learn a lot about him. Instead by the end of the Rotary program I truly felt as if I had met him. It was powerful, inspiring, and surprisingly endearing. In fact, it made me proud to be an American. And along with everyone in that room our applause felt like applause for our twenty-sixth president, not the impersonator standing before us.

In the end, Holy Revelation is not about learning the Bible but learning to meet, to love, and to trust the Lord Jesus Christ to whom the Bible introduces us. As Jesus tells us, "I am the way, the truth, and the life" (John 14:6). Like that impersonator, the goal of Scripture is to reveal the inner character of Christ so that we will know him as our dear friend, Lord, and Master.

The Bible introduced Christ to me, but I have come to truly know him better and better through others. Every time a new aspect is revealed my heart sings, my faith soars, and my commitment to him is deepened. As Holy Revelation continues to reveal the character of Christ to me, my faith, my love, and my awe for him has grown.

WHAT CAN CHURCHES DO TO CULTIVATE THE EXPERIENCE OF GOD THROUGH HOLY REVELATION?

The challenge for pastors is the reality that by and large the sermon is not the place in worship where people experience God, at least not in Presbyterian churches. Though these focus group participants greatly admired their pastors personally, and found their sermons enriching, the sermon was rarely cited as a source of experiencing God's presence.

I believe this has a great deal to do with our training and our traditions. Despite the instinct of most Presbyterian clergy, I don't think our theology is truly a barrier to a way of preaching that connects people deeply to God's presence. Having said that, it would require dramatic shifts in preaching style which would prove problematic at first. For this shift, it might be best for us to turn to known examples from within our denomination or at least preachers from other denominations which share our theology.

The default, of course, is telling a story. But frankly, sometimes that feels like cheating, lacking imagination, and selling short our literary styles.

Perhaps the best example I have seen in this regard comes from an African-American professor of preaching. He was not of the Presbyterian tradition but has taught many PCUSA preachers.

One of his students invited him to preach at her installation at a prominent progressive, but very traditional, predominantly Anglo church in Atlanta. Like most Presbyterian churches, mine included, applause is never given in worship, not for the choir, not even for the children's choirs. After all, music is worship offered to God and not the glory of the singers. It certainly makes sense to me.

But something happened at the end of the sermon that still shocks me to this day. Those seven hundred people erupted in applause—not the kind in which a few people begin, and peer pressure leads others to chime in. No! It was spontaneous and completely from the heart.

I believe they were not so much applauding the pastor as they never would have done such a thing, but they were exploding with the joy at discovering the power of God from their hearts and this, like having your knee knocked by your doctor, was an instinctual reaction that no one could control!

As I reflect on the pastor's preaching style and content, it was unique. It was filled with excellent and insightful content, outstanding in fact, but not world-shatteringly insightful.

But his style added something special. He preached with a vibrant, joyous energy that embodied the sense of the "good news" he was preaching about. When coupled with his reflective and erudite examination, the truth leaped past our frozen-chosen defenses and lit up our spines (and hands!) with life.

Learning this approach would take time but would truly help people experience God's truth more powerfully in our preaching.

HOLY LOVE: A SENSE OF UNCONDITIONAL ACCEPTANCE BY GOD, FOR OTHERS AND FOR YOURSELF, AND A FEELING OF PROFOUND CARE AND DEVOTION

For God so loved the world...

JOHN 3:16A

With the endless judgments in our world and the many personal failures people have experienced, there is an urgent need for unconditional love.

This love often appeared in surprising ways. One woman was participating in a devotional exercise at a Christian camp. At first it seemed corny and hokey. "Close your eyes and picture Jesus." She was a teacher, so she pictured him as a little boy. So, the director said, "Ask him to come over to you. Ask him a question." At this point she is thinking, "How ridiculous!" But she played along.

Since he grew up to be a carpenter, she pictured this boy in the carpenter's shop, bare footed, covered in dust, and carving on a piece of wood, very intent on getting it just right.

So, she asked him, "What are you making, because you're working so hard on that?"

And he said, "This is you."

As she continued, suddenly all the other people in the room did not make a hill of beans difference. She said, "You are working so hard on that I must be a lot of trouble."

And he said, "No, this is my joy."

As she shared this story, I suddenly felt that same love of God for me. It had never occurred to me that all the trouble I make for God and all the tweaking God does in the world is not a burden, but a joy. This cast a new light on all the terrors of the world, for it put all of them in the carpenter's hands, which are fully capable of shaping us, me, and everything into God's intentions. It also gave me a sense of assurance of God's love; for Jesus' dutiful carving upon me will never end until it is complete. It let me see that all our problems are fully manageable in the divine hands of love.

Another participant experienced the love of God while seeing, of all things, a hat. Her daughter was a volunteer in mission on the West Coast, and her East Coast church had a knitting ministry. While visiting the mission at which her daughter worked, a woman walked toward her wearing one of the hats while saying, "Your church gave me this hat!" The mother told me, "Seeing that knitted hat was seeing God's love." When I asked her to elaborate, she explained that it showed her that God loves us enough to use us in ways that matter, finds surprising ways to connect us all to each other, and finally that God's care for those in need is ever present.

Unsurprisingly, mission trips were a source of knowing God's love, but not always in ways you would expect. One focus group member described an encounter with a young girl.

> I remember it most from my first Dominican Republic trip . . . There are kids everywhere. All the time they want to play and talk. There was an eight-year-old girl who showed me her music book. Suddenly, in a deeper way, I realized God wants the same thing for this girl and my first-world daughter . . . and that is why we are here; That was a very profound moment; to look in those girl's eyes. . . . It is the same, no separation by culture, color, wealth. . . . God wants nothing less for her.

The stories that people shared continuously disclosed that those moments of loving others, whether stranger, friend, or family, had deep impact on their being. The power of these simple stories showed me just how much it is missing from our daily lives in general.

Another person makes a deliberate effort to express love for others because that was what she was taught to do. She normally does a morning devotion, but during Lent she decided to change it up.

> We did not give up things for Lent, so I wanted to do something intentional to let people know I was thinking about them . . . sharing times that we have had together. Each morning I wrote a note . . . to someone every day . . . I wrote to people I knew well or did not know very well at all. . . . One of my college friends told me that her wife wept with joy when she read it. I simply said that I was supportive of their relationship and I was grateful that she found someone to love. That was why she wept.

This woman's story showed me the importance of expressing our hearts to others. It can impact people in ways that go beyond our understanding. It can connect people to that love of God we all yearn for.

> The consistent theme
> through everyone's experience,
> the thread that was woven
> into all their stories,
> was an overpowering sense
> of God's unconditional acceptance
> and overwhelming LOVE.

The Scriptures are various but the central one is found in John 3:16–17 and we only need a few words to convey so much,

    God SO loved the WORLD.

Like many of you I have been familiar with this verse since I was a child but parts of it gained deeper meaning during my sabbatical. . . . The world. God loves the world. God loves everyone.

    I knew God so loved the world,
    but when you see it,
    in travels through the country
    and around the world,
    and meet people,
    just people,
    who live and die,
    who eat and breathe,
    who ache and hope,
    who share
    the deepest yearnings of their heart
    and those moments in which they knew
    the blessed assurance
    of divine devotion,
    affection, and tenderness . . .
    . . . when you see it,
    you realize God has
    so much more going on,
        in your street,
            your neighborhood,
                your town,
                    the state,
                        the country,
    AND THE PLANET!
than you can ever imagine.
And in an amazing way it assures you of God's love and care for your own situation and needs.
If God is paying so much attention
to all the different corners of the world,
surely God is doing the same for you.
As you hear these stories
you hear God's passionate, hungry,
yearning, aching love for them.

And people can experience this care in even the briefest of encounters.

During one church gathering people were sharing their stories. After a man shared a story of failure and loss another man came to him and simply said, "I've been right there. In that same hard place." To someone witnessing that event it felt like those were words from God, an expression of God's sympathy and God's parental care, not simply that man's kindness and these stories came from every kind person in any moment.

> The world teaches us
> to love certain people . . .
> those who look like us
> and act like us,
> who share our same beliefs,
> but in these stories,
> it became oh so clear!
> God makes no such choices!
> Jesus said,
> "If you love those who love you
> of what credit is that?
> Do not even the hypocrites do the same?!"

The whole world Jesus speaks of is not a metaphor, or mere description. If God sees no need to pick and choose then neither should I.

But even more wonderfully, in a way that only God could accomplish, God's love is not only universal, covering the whole planet, but we also find it very personal and intimate. Jesus calls his disciples friends and he teaches us to pray to God as a heavenly parent.

But we have put up barriers to knowing this type of love. God uses others to convey it, yet we are afraid of making ourselves vulnerable because we are afraid of being judged and dismissed.

When we are willing to peel back the layers of defense, we will know the Lord's tender and passionate love for us. This became clear to me in one person's story. He described a church mission trip:

> At the end of the trip we gather as a group and everybody shares.
> It is voluntary but almost everyone does.

At this moment his voice broke. He paused to compose himself and as he continued you could hear in his voice and see in his eyes that it was a deep, intimate moment of speaking about something very personal, very profound, very loving, and very sacred:

> You pick someone in the group and use this phrase, "Jesus is the light of the world and I see that light in you." . . . And you say

to them how you saw God working in them that week. It is a highlight of [my] spiritual life.

I heard dozens of these stories everywhere I went. and I realized you and I have these powerful feelings of love for a moment and they overwhelm us. But God's love is always on full throttle.

The Bible uses the word "steadfast" to describe this love. And it is a tireless, unrelenting love that does not wax and wane with the Lord's mood or our misdeeds. It is most clearly seen in God's chosen people, the Jews. Throughout the Old Testament the Israelites fall away from worshiping the Lord, abuse the poor, and fail the commandments. It infuriates and frustrates God. But God does not abandon them.

God will never abandon them.

And so, the psalmist gives praise, "O give thanks to the God of heaven, for his steadfast love endures forever" (Psalm 136:26).

Some saw this steadfastness through observing others. For one person it happened at children's time. As she watched the children come forward, she noticed a parent that came forward to sit close, "to make sure he's okay." Seeing the parent's care reminded her of God's unwavering care. God gives us freedom to fully live in the world, but God is always close at hand, ready to step in.

As I listened to these stories it led my mind to wander in an unexpected direction. Cake!

In the fall of 2018, I was visiting my mother and she pulled out a magazine. It had this picture of a cake, and a recipe she wanted me to bake. I had not baked much in years but after glancing at it, my mouth was already watering, and I was game!

> The layered buttercream frosting was exciting!
> The tiered fudge cake was enticing!
> But the gooey, creamy, chocolatey
> ganache icing was intoxicating!
> It was sugar, cream, and chocolate,
> injected with a jillion megawatts of electric delight!!

As people described God's love it seemed that they had experienced this same extravagant overabundance of joy. Like the parable of the prodigal son in which the father throws a blowout party for his son that has returned. "There is more joy in heaven over one sinner that repents!"

But there is another side to this love of God that goes beyond moments of joy and instances of blessings. Like any good parent God not only provides the comfort but the discipline and sacrifice necessary.

Thus, Jesus continues his words, "God so loved the world . . . that he gave his only Son." Steadfast love that will not let go is a divine joy . . . and burden.

> Love can make us miserable.
> We worry about our parents,
> our uncle;
> our friend.
> The Bible tells us
> that God's love was so painful
> that it cut the divine heart.
> For to love someone is to be in pain they are in pain.
> To love someone is to be hungry when they are hungry,
> to be sad when they are sad.
> So, God's love must be excruciatingly painful;
> for I know how painful it can sometimes be
> to love my two children,
> but Jesus knows that kind of love
> for every person,
> and he felt it all
> when God gave him,
> the only begotten Son,
> to the cross.
> Jesus felt it all for us.

There was one focus group that paid special emphasis to this aspect of God's love. They objected to the incessant talk of God's unconditional love because to them it sounded like God did not care about how we lived, treated others, or observed God's laws. With the endless judgments in our world and the many personal failures people have experienced there is an urgent need for unconditional love. As Paul said, love never ends. But sometimes this is confused with God's love being soft or easy like an overly permissive parent.

In fact, most of the time God's love is less like the *Leave It to Beaver* father and more like a relentless mother (did any of you have one of those?) who won't leave us alone in the corner to be less than she knows we are capable of.

As Malachi explains, "For he is like a refiner's fire, he will sit as a refiner and purifier of silver, and he will purify the descendants of Levi and refine them like gold and silver, until they present offerings to the Lord in righteousness" (Malachi 3:3).

In other words, God is not going to give up on us and God is going to keep working on us until God has refined all the dross from our souls and they realize their full shining purity.

Hebrews uses the parent metaphor to convey the same message,

> My child do not regard lightly the discipline of the Lord, or lose heart when you are punished by him; for the Lord disciplines those whom he loves, and chastises every child whom he accepts. (Hebrews 12:5b–6)

There is, however, another unique type of love I found not on this journey, but on another one with fellow clergy that led us to a Catholic monastery in Alabama.

When we Protestants experience love, it always seems to be relational—with a subject, the one doing the loving, and the object, the one being loved. Although powerful, this makes love transactional.

There is something the Catholics experience that is rarely found in Protestant churches, much less Presbyterian ones. In fact, I had not even conceived of this type of love until I heard a Catholic brother describe his daily devotional Bible reading, in which he reads one or two verses. He said, "After about two hours . . ."

Two hours, with one verse! I couldn't imagine that much patience, but when he continued, his next words will stay with me forever: "It was like being assumed into a sapphire light." The beauty of the phrase made my soul yearn for such a moment.

As I heard him explain this further, I realized he was not feeling loved, but he was feeling love. Love's essence. In fact, since God is love, he was experiencing God's essence, the stuff that makes God . . . God. It is the difference between taking a sip of water and leaping into and being surrounded by it. It is the difference between seeing a beam of light illuminate your next step through the dark and being enveloped in the radiant light of the sun.

WHAT CAN THE CHURCH DO TO FOSTER HOLY LOVE?

The focus group conversations disclosed a need for an important distinction when we speak of God's love. As I mentioned earlier, one focus group objected to all this talk of unconditional love because to them it sounded like unconditional acceptance.

In other words, for them the church sometimes gives people the idea that what that their actions and beliefs are is of no consequence to God because no matter what, God will accept you.

> So, the challenge is for us to explain
> that no matter what,
> God will love us;
> but that does not mean,
> God does not demand everything of us,
> and furthermore,
> our beliefs and actions
> matter a great deal to our Lord.

Holding the two together without compromise, God's unswerving love for everyone and God's demand for us to follow the divine will forge a more believable and compelling path to follow. Too often we lean so heavily on one side that people turn away or turn us off. Twitter is the clearest example of run-away hateful judgment. The church must not reflect that type of call to the will of God. It must not make demons out of faulty humans. We need to teach society how to, in Pauline fashion, "speak the truth . . . in love."

HOLY GIFTS, HOLY PURPOSE: EXPERIENCING GOD THROUGH A SENSE OF DIVINE PURPOSE IN YOUR LIFE GROWING FROM A SENSE OF USEFULNESS FOR GOD'S PLAN

To each is given the manifestation of the Spirit for the common good.

1 CORINTHIANS 12:7

Whether at home or away, people want their lives to make a difference.

> But there is a struggle . . .
> ironically, in this age of frenetic activity,
> we are traveling more,
> working longer hours,
> shuffling children to more activities,
> caring for parents with greater energy
> than ever before in the history of the world;
> . . . but there is a struggle to feel like any of it has purpose.

People of faith have an answer to this conundrum. Serve Christ, love others, worship the Lord. But for many, knowing this is not enough. There is still a void of meaning.

Midlife crisis has existed for a long time now, but this void of meaning has seeped down even into the twentysomethings. But perhaps the greatest challenge is for those in their later years.

So many lose the feeling of purpose upon retirement or loss of a spouse. Many, many times people have shared the heartbreaking feeling with me, that they simply don't know why God hasn't taken them to heaven yet, because they no longer feel of any use in this world.

But the good news comes from stories across all ages of profound purpose from simple moments. During my research I encountered people of every age surprised by being used by God to bless others which leads us to our next mode of experience in our series: Holy Gifts, Holy Purpose.

Justice ministries is a critical place where many churches connect people to the gifts they have for bringing about God's will. Whether it is writing their legislatures, standing on the Capitol steps, or speaking out against racism and hatred, when people can use their voice for God's truth, it can be an electrifying experience. Of course, this can be a highly polarizing topic in churches. The challenge is being able to speak God's bold, prophetic truth while not becoming captive to the same noisy, self-righteous posturing we see everywhere.

One young person experienced God in the gathering of young people.

> My generation wants to make a difference. And when we all come together and talk about making changes in the world for the better, I can't better see how God is using me, them and all of us.

Once again, the Scripture is simple brief and to the point. This time our guidance comes from Paul and it is another text, despite whatever level of faith we may have, we refuse to believe: Each has been given a spiritual gift for the common good . . . 1 Corinthians 12:7.

Much of people's lack of purpose comes from a common dis-ease in our world—people lack confidence, confidence in their ability to do things that matter. This lack of confidence is different from humility. Humility is "whatever I can do, I can only do it 'through him who strengthens me,'" but the belief that "I have no particular skill or talent" is really the denial of the word of God and God's power.

Paul insists that God has bestowed something special in the heart, mind, body, and soul of every single person. Furthermore, it is through this gift that God's plan for the world unfolds!

Now identifying this gift is not something we can always do ourselves because a spiritual gift is not necessarily an innate talent . . . though it can be. Take the disciples for instance.

Jesus did not choose those who were successful in the world. Rather he chose ordinary people, not well-known, not of great wealth or poverty, just average folks, the ones who disappear by the billions into the lost memory of time; the people about whom no historian or novelist would ever write; except that they encountered the Christ and used whatever they had to God's purposes and so had the most profound impact of any twelve ever.

Sometimes to serve Christ we need to suppress our natural talents. The apostle Paul's talent in the world was intellectual rigor, religious zeal, and dogged pursuit . . . but it turned out the devil is the one who used those for his purposes.

But after Damascus, Paul realized God did not want him to use his intellectual rigor. As he tells us, he became foolish. "My proclamation [was] not with plausible words of wisdom." Though drafted into professional baseball, my father left those skills behind to serve the gospel.

In the end, the distinction between a spiritual gift and a talent is quite simple: whenever people experience God through you, your talent becomes a spiritual gift. A further exploration will show that a spiritual gift benefits

> the common good,
> to the glory of God,
> by the power of God.

We shall examine each aspect in turn beginning with Paul's assertion that a spiritual gift benefits the common good.

The Common Good . . .

It is how you use the talent that makes the difference. A talent to make money can be a regular gift for your life, but if it is used for a fundraiser for cancer suddenly it is being used for the common good. The gift of cooking barbecue can be a tremendous blessing not only to our taste buds but for the fellowship that surrounds it.

And even the simplest of actions in key moments can make a great difference. A person might have the gift of conversation and could easily use it to spread gossip. But Wendy and I had a waitress that has served us many times recently say, "I just love married couples! Ya'll are so great together!" That little comment brightened our day in a powerful way! Her observation blessed us!

Sometimes a spiritual gift might be a skill you have used your whole life but one day in a confounding and frustrating moment God opens your eyes. It is not always a feeling of the heart but sometimes a realization of the mind. At least that is how it was for one young teacher I interviewed.

She is in her late twenties and teaches in a very challenging environment.

> There were moments as a first-year teacher . . . I have students with drugs, in gangs, who have their only meal at school, they try you and try you each day; I should feel for them, but you are angry, but then the anger reminds you . . . *that is the reason you are there.*

It was precisely in the hardship and horror of drugs and pre-teen pregnancies, the stark reality of broken lives, that assured her God had placed her there. She has thick skin and stubborn resolve. That is what God needed there. Because if it was easy anyone could do it.

The experience of using these spiritual gifts for the common good leads to the next powerful moment in the divine plan: the glory of God.

To the Glory of God

One retiree from a focus group experienced the typical moment of losing his sense of purpose. He was a businessman in his professional life. He never had a sense that his job had any more purpose than putting food on his family's table which was fine with him. Now, he had always liked working with his hands and over the years had done various projects around the house. So, when someone invited him to volunteer for Habitat for Humanity he said "yes."

> And, for the first time in his life,
> after seventy years,
> he experienced a sense of Holy Purpose
> in his actions through his gifts.

After a few months' work, he attended the dedication when the house is given over to the proud new owner, and it profoundly touched him. She introduced her boys and explained how this house would be a safe place to call home. She was the first in her family to own a house, and her tears flowed freely, as she was filled with profound thanksgiving for all those who made it possible.

As he listened, he felt touched not only by having a purpose but by being used as the hands of God to do sacred work in the world. The hands of God! What could be more energizing in all the world! Suddenly, his own tears were flowing as his heart sung praises to God for being used in such an awesome fashion. He saw the glory of God come about through the work of his hands and it knocked him flat!

Finally, as we use these gifts for the common good to the glory of God, on a rare occasion we feel that all of it is happening by the power of God!

By the Power of God

This is what Paul meant when he wrote, "I can do all things through him who strengthens me." He realized when he abandoned his need to argue through his intellectual prowess that God was working through him—not by his skill, but by his lack of skill!

> It is in these moments
> that you have a keen awareness
> that it is God
> who is literally,
> consciously,
> actively
> using
> . . . YOU.

Not a generic intellectual realization, no, not at all. It is an experience of being a conduit of the divine intentions. Something like when you touch the static electric ball and your hair rises up. It is in seeing the effect that you know something is flowing through you and not you doing it. God can create this delight with any gift or skill.

Some have gifts they don't see as divine because it is simply what they do in daily life. One Charleston college professor was caught off guard when a fellow church member asked him to help her write her obituary. She was dying and did not know him or the pastor of the church very well at all.

The request was a surprise, not only because he had no interactions with her, but he had never done anything like this in his life. He presumed she asked because he taught English. During the visit they came to know one another, and indeed it was clear she had only a few days left. They decided not only to write the obituary but plan her funeral as well. Again, something he had never done.

Though she was not a regular attender it became clear that she could use a visit from the pastor and a final communion as well. The pastor, professor, and another elder came to her room and together they shared the sacred meal. At the end she lifted her hands and with enthusiasm and clarity beyond her physical condition she declared, "I am ready to go!" And a few hours later she died.

This professor is clearly more of an intellectual and academic person not prone to these experiences in his daily life. So being used by God in this fashion and in this way was a life-altering moment and a profound affirmation of the providence of God.

Paul wrote, "Each has been given a gift for the common good," and that means you. So be ready; at any time in any way God might use you! And you too will know the electric joy of serving this wondrous God!

What Can Churches do to Help People Experience Holy Gifts and Purpose?

Many congregations have done gift surveys and volunteer sign-ups. Occasionally they work well, but often, there is little gain for the effort. Perhaps a greater adaptability to unique moments and the unique gifts of members might address those needs. This would require strong relationships with congregants to better understand the gifts God has given them.

A greater focus on people's life stages can help as well. Retirees and empty nesters often have both lost purpose and more time. Many empty nesters drift away from church. These are often the same parents who were here every time the doors of the church opened. Then the kids graduate, and they are gone.

Churches need to be much more intentional about this transition. One afternoon a member and I were looking at the directory. As we perused the names and faces, she said, "Once they get their kids through . . . they just leave; they don't feel compelled to come. . . . They go to the beach." It is critical to better understand this group. They have not left the church. They are not angry. But for some reason, without their children, church is not a compelling place for them to be. Somehow, we should be able to find a way to connect them to God more powerfully at this phase in their lives.

HOLY PROVIDENCE: AN EXPERIENCE OF GOD AT WORK IN THE WORLD; GOD'S PROVIDENTIAL POWER AND GOD'S HOLY TIMING

We know that all things work together for good for those who love God.

ROMANS 8:28

"It was God's plan." "It was God's will." "God led me here." These are phrases I hear all the time in my ministry. My seminary training taught me to be skeptical of such phrases. After all, how can people know? Additionally, once you study the history of atrocities and prejudicial acts (like suicide cults and the Crusades) all committed all in the name of the divine plan such talk feels presumptuous at best and self-serving at worst! Especially the crass statements people make to parents about car accidents and birth defects being God's will.

And yet, despite the accuracy of such challenges, on my sabbatical journey I found a persistent, clear, and deep sense from people all over the country that God is very much in control. People from many educational, economic, and racial backgrounds persistently see God intimately working in their personal lives and the world.

For a time in my life, I dismissed the idea of providence. Not so much because I didn't believe in it but because trying to pull apart the threads of God's will and human apathy and evil was simply too complicated and too susceptible to our infinite capacity to rationalize.

I realize I can no longer justify backing off from this doctrine. It is too deeply intertwined with the hallmark of Reformed thought, it is too pervasive in Scripture, and in a way, I made it too easy for myself, and if there is one thing the Bible teaches us about faith . . . it is never easy!

> Providence is rooted in the great doctrine of the Sovereignty of God,
> a sovereignty and control so powerful and so pervasive
> that you must say it with all capitals,
> with a low, thunderous voice
> that suggests its potency in the speaking of it,
> THE SOVEREIGNTY OF GOD!

In other words, God is in control . . . of everything! "God," says John Calvin, "is keeper of the keys and therefore governs all events."[1] God is in control not only of the course of history and the grand contours of time but of your life and mine. And when it comes to benevolent intent for humanity, it is referred to as the providence of God.

In Paul's letter to the Romans he lays all on the line: "All things work together for good, for those who love God."

The very design behind the universe discloses God's providential care for us. Jesus tells his disciples not to be anxious, because just like God provides for the birds of the air, which neither toil nor spin, so too does God's beneficent hand work to provide our needs but out of even greater love and care. God designed this world so that we would have food to eat, air to breathe, and water to drink. Every apple you crunch, every breath you take, and every sip of water is literally a gift from God.

When God provided the ram at the last minute to spare Isaac from sacrifice, a new name for God was born, *Jehovah Jireh*, God the provider. The ancient Hebrews had a keen understanding that everything from nature that sustained their lives was a direct blessing from God.

---

2. Calvin, *Institutes*, 1.16.4.

But God knows,
(God always knows!)
our infinite capacity
to turn anything and everything
into an idol,
to treat things
as God.

So, amazingly God's providence,
God's love for us,
God's actions in history,
even use
the absence of these blessings
for our own good.

This means as wonderful as God's providence is, at times it is most tiresome. I am sure that Abraham would have preferred that God's providence would have never led him up that mountain with Isaac to begin with. But that is not how God works. And so, God shoves the whole Israelite nation into the wilderness . . . to train them into trust.

Deuteronomy tells us,

> He humbled you by letting you hunger, then by feeding you with manna, with which neither you nor your ancestors were acquainted, in order to make you understand that one does not live by bread alone, but by every word that comes from the mouth of the Lord. (Deuteronomy 8:3)

And it is such spiritual training from God that gave Paul the strength to write these words,

> "My grace is sufficient for you, for power is made perfect in weakness." So, I will boast all the more gladly of my weaknesses, so that the power of Christ may dwell in me. Therefore I am content with weaknesses, insults, hardships, persecutions, and calamities for the sake of Christ; for whenever I am weak, then I am strong. (2 Corinthians 9:10–12)

Paul was a freak,
an aberration, an anomaly!
When I am weak, I am strong!?
(Who talks like that?)
Content with calamities!
Insults! Persecutions!

> (Are you kidding me!
> When I feel weak
> I . . . feel . . . weak!!!!
> The opposite of strong!)
> How! How did Paul do it?
> . . . Love.
> (You're kidding me, right?!)
> No,
> "All things work together for good for those who LOVE God."
> Providence doesn't work without loving trust.

If we don't turn to God in times of hardship with loving trust, then trials will simply be miserable moments that break us down. That is why it's called faith. Because we must believe where we have not seen. We must trust no matter where life takes us.

One person I interviewed shared God's delightfully dastardly and devious sense of humor. She encountered God's providence when she was actively trying to avoid it. She changed churches and when she did, she was determined not to get involved because she had gotten too busy at her previous one:

> I have been Presbyterian for only five years, and I thought to myself, "I am going to do nothing in this church. . . ." But it does not let you do that; you have all these wonderful friends; they are very sneaky. . . . God is so at work in this church; he puts the right people in your path; and I know he put them there, and all my plans were in the garbage can!

The garbage can might just be the best place for them! For there is one word in this Romans passage that has always bothered me. It is the very first word. And I hate it!

> All,
> All things!
> All things work together for good!
> Can God's sovereign power
> possibly be that strong,
> that wise,
> that pervasive?
>
> Having to write about providence
> makes me feel like the doctor
> who must go under the knife
> and discover how scary and painful

surgery and recovery can be!

This faith is hard work.

Some of you might think pastors are more faithful and trusting
and that is why we are called to ministry.
It is the opposite.
It is because we need the focus
to constantly remind ourselves
of God's providential love!

And so, in the end, I know
if we submit to any of it,
we must submit to all of it,
which means
that in some way,
beyond my knowing
and my perception,
that the fact that my house on Partridge
has not sold yet
is,
by some inscrutable means
(utterly opaque to me!),
part of God's good and beneficent plan!
Victor Hugo said it very well,
"Above all,
you can believe in Providence
in either of two ways,
either as thirst believes in the orange,
or as the ass believes in the whip." —Victor Hugo[2]

We would love for providence to be endless oranges, juicy sweet and sublime. But God loves you and me too much!

As a result, there is a plethora of simple yet powerful stories of people experiencing the providence of God. Often the realization that God has arranged events comes as a welcome surprise at times of drudgery. After a long day volunteering at the hospital, a woman was ready to go home. It had seemed an almost pointless day. But one last visit made all the difference and another volunteer said to her, "That is why we were here today."

She explained to me that she felt deep inside that God had specifically sent her on that day to that person at exactly the right time. This was a regular refrain through the focus groups. God was not only present in a general

2. Hugo, *The Man Who Laughs*, 10.

sense, but intimately concerned about every detail. Like a good parent, God is involved but not controlling. When this experience is coupled with being able to play a part and not simply being an observer, it magnifies the experience of God many times.

People saw God's providence at work in worship as well. "It seems like things just always come together." "The song was just what I needed." "A particular person on a particular day sings a particular song. It must be the hand of God!"

We might be tempted to think this is all about mere personal preference, but I don't think so. One participant spoke of attending a different service:

> At early service today, I tend to be more traditional, but I went to the less formal one . . . there was solo I had never heard. . . . It was sung from his heart. It was beautiful. It was as if he had written it. He sung it as if it came out from his story and some of it is reflected in his story, and so that made it more powerful.

He experienced this moment as the providence of God because of how perfectly it came together.

I was most surprised that people even saw the providence of God in committees, even the finance committee! About serving on the committee for years, one man declared, "The numbers just seem to always work out." Many times, they had to trust in faith that the finances of the church would work at year's end even though the numbers indicated the opposite. "Does that mean all the money always comes in?" I asked.

> No, but you have to be positive about it even if it does not work. Just don't be negative. . . . It's not easy to convince people to be positive. There will be a time when we can make the adjustments. And we do. So, you see, it always works out.

Pastors often experience the providence of God through visitation. We know we can't possibly visit everyone or know when people need it the most. So, when the timing is just right, we know God is at work. One pastor said, "I went to visit a member with cancer, and she said, 'I was hoping you would come today.' She died the next day. God sent us there." Perhaps in ways church members will never know, hearing those words from our members is like hearing the voice of God. He said, "The hair stood up on my neck and tears flowed out of my eyes. I was saying thank you God for sending me out here; it was tears of gratitude."

We pastors are faulty, misguided people, stumbling in the dark ourselves while trying to show people the light of God. And occasionally, when we get it just right, it makes it all worth it.

What Can the Church Do to Help People Experience the Providence of God?

In many of these stories the person is a passive observer, but not always. One person described a recent service.

> Someone came to worship today who has not been in a while . . . who has been through horrible things this year and I thought the sermon was perfect . . .just what that person needed to hear that day. It was a witness to me that God is at work in helping that person.

But this observer did not remain passive. God nudged her to act. She said,

> I am in the choir and saw her face, then went and spoke to her, and I wanted to listen, and she was going through some of the things I was aware of. She had a lot of problems; I wanted to listen.

To teach our members to become participants in God's providential action will multiply their experience of God, like ripples in a pond. This means teaching them the biblical story. It shows them how to recognize God's movement and gives them examples of when and how to dive in. I know one Presbyterian church that has begun doing testimonies again to accomplish this.

HOLY GRACE: EXPERIENCING GOD'S WONDROUS MERCY AND HEALING PRESENCE IN TIMES OF PERSONAL CRISIS, HARDSHIP, OR TRAGEDY

Grace to you and peace from God our father and the Lord Jesus Christ.

Philippians 1:2

When times are at their worst, people experience God the most powerfully. Of course, we know that many do not. This can make hard times even worse.
    About year ago, a beloved member of a church passed away after a long, hard-fought illness. For his wife, it was a tremendous, lonesome burden and a heartbreaking loss. But someone, an angel if you will, sent her a message. It was Hebrews 13:5, "I will never leave or forsake you," along with just a few words, "I am stamping this on my heart and claiming this promise for you!" This message of God's care from a friend during a very difficult time was a source of great angelic comfort. God gave her grace through this woman's simple kindness.

One pastor described the grace of simply being present with those who are dying.

> It is hard for people to understand how precious it is to be with people when they die, such an honor to help them walk through the transition . . . how powerfully God is present in the room. I have had more than one experience where the person conveyed, they saw someone come to get them, or say I am ready, and they are so peaceful. They were suffering so badly until that moment and they find peace.

For one who has deep faith, that moment of death after hours, weeks, months, years of suffering is the grace of being released from drowning into the glorious, stratified air of eternal life with God.

One person looked for a practical respite for his grieving sister. She had lost her daughter.

> The one thing that would really help my sister . . . she said, "would be to get a swim in . . . but the swim team takes up the whole pool." I met the director of the YMCA and right away he said, "If there is anything I can do let me know." Suddenly, my sister had an hour . . .
>
> As the closest thing to a pastor my family had, I was to give the message. It felt like the darkest morning ever in the history of the world. . . . Then a friend texted and said, "I have been praying for you and you are all prayed up." I knew I could not sing, I teared up . . . didn't think I could do it. Then I remembered the text and I thought, yes, I could do it.

This man felt God's grace in tragedy by being made strong enough to be there for his family, and that strength came from a friend back home who simply took the time to send a few heartfelt words in a text. It only takes the smallest gesture to open the sublime light of God's love in dark times.

Another person finds this grace in debate with God. She has a physical challenge and, like most anyone, at times she feels bitter. That is when she gets feisty.

> Sometimes I argue with God when I am angry. . . . God why me! . . . But once I give up, everything is good. . . . When I give in, I am okay. . . . Who do you want to have it . . . the sickness . . . and I think about all these wonderful people . . . and I realize its okay that it is me.

Another person learned this same attitude from a friend that had A.L.S.

> My former partner spoke about a CEO with A.L.S.... Two weeks later he was diagnosed with the disease as well.... He said, "Why not me?"... I learned it is okay to question and be angry, but not everyone is.

This person's matter-of-fact approach to their disease showed another man grace in discovering that not all challenges have to define how we perceive our life.

Another person had the same experience with her mother's death.

> Sometimes I have experienced God when I am angry at God.... I watched my mother die with a terribly degrading disease.... If there ever was a godly woman, this was it. How could she stay positive and how angry I was... that Romans verse, "All works together."... You may not understand the disease, but you have to believe there is good that come out of it.

Seeing her mother's unswerving faith in her agony showed her that, even then, God's love shines through. If her mom believed, that was enough to convince her.

Family can either be especially helpful or especially hurtful in hard times and often both, but when a family sticks together in love even then it can lead to God's grace, as this same woman explained.

> Watching her as a role model, through her death and after her death, while she was going through it... I was the major caregiver. It was just seeing how God used that whole situation to help my sister and I build bridges with each other; it was amazing the good that came out of it.... My sister and I... we are total opposites. She is not a believer; but we discussed politics and she came at it from a hopeless point of view;... she is a good-hearted person.... My mother waited 'til we were all there until she died... and I felt God and she thought, "Since we were all there, it is time for me to go to God."... It was peaceful but never easy.... Mine is not anger, but in not understanding you have to have faith. Faith that God's plan is higher than our thoughts.

In those times when people are able to hang on long enough, for a wedding, a birthday, or simply for a chance to say goodbye to everyone, God's grace is known in this simple knowledge of knowing they have been given a special moment to hold as a memory in the absence to come. The extra time is seen as a gift from God and a source of profound gratitude.

People don't always expect everything to be perfect, so they can see God in the special gifts during hardship.

Just What Is Grace?

Many religions emphasize love and even those without any religion see its merit. But the type of love that Christians speak of is a radically alien way of treating other people and its disappearing in this world, most pointedly seen in the scorched earth mentality found in the news pundits and the social media clowns.

Name calling is part of the problem in the world, so I apologize but I call them clowns not just to be derogatory but to point to their essence.

> A clown is someone
> who looks like a person,
> but with exaggerated features:
> an extra wide smile,
> big red nose,
> oversized feet,
> and rather insane actions.

The clown's purpose is to exaggerate in order to evoke a reaction.
The clown's purpose is to evoke laughter,
but many social media minions' purposes are more nefarious
—to exaggerate our baser emotions
of hatred, judgment, separatism, and more.

Perhaps most disconcerting of all are those Christians who use these same methods to justify any kind of behavior in order to support their own goals. But what they and all the others fail to realize is what is so amazing about grace. All the social problems in this world can be understood through our failure to know and live grace.

But we don't really know what grace is . . .

> Grace is elegance and poise in movement.
> . . . Grace is good manners in civil society.
> . . . Grace is a prayer before a meal.
> . . . Grace is an extended period before repayment of a loan.
> With all these different types of grace we might be forgiven for failing to realize what its essence is.

For the essence of grace IS the essence of God.

Grace perhaps more than any other word in all of Scripture captures the core of the Lord Jesus Christ, his unique calling, and the nature of his love.

Grace is not a provisional measure you apply at certain times.
Grace was not a temporary tactic God used on the cross.
It is always the right time for grace.
Especially when those who oppose you employ the baser tactics.

So, when the world was at its worst,
Christ took it upon himself,
not fighting,
not cursing,
not getting down on their level;
he took it all,
every last nail,
until before his last breath he prayed,
"Father, forgive them."
Grace is that moment in which you receive love and kindness
when what you deserve is a reprimand or a punishment.

The text is drawn once again from Paul,

"Grace to you and peace from God our father and the Lord Jesus Christ."

Perhaps out of all the other moments of God this one catches you off guard, surprises your heart, and makes you gasp for air from the unexpected wonder of it all!

It is often brief moments of being reminded of our loved ones that this rush of grace comes because they remind us of all the good things that we had. It makes us gasp for breath because up until this moment we had been sucking air through a straw . . .

This past year I was privileged to be a part of a hospital program in which you spend nine months learning more about Spartanburg Regional Hospital System and if you are lucky, even take a ride in the emergency helicopter. But one tour truly enabled me to feel empathy for the sick.

For a few moments (not even minutes) we had to breathe through a straw to mimic the stress of having to breathe on a vent to better understand what those with C.O.P.D. and other lung problems experience twenty-four hours a day.

It only took a few labored breaths
until I began to feel

> deprived of oxygen,
> lightheaded,
> and a rising panic.
> As I listened to people's experience of grace it seemed like a type suffocation they were experiencing.
> But instead of lack of oxygen,
> it was lack of health,
> love,
> and most of all hope.
> It became clear
> that part of experiencing the grace of God
> is first knowing its absence.
>
> It is the Christ on the cross,
> crying out in horror,
> at the God who abandon him.
>
> But when that trickle of Holy Spirit power
> becomes a flood of God's love,
> the rush of it
> makes you swoon
> and praise
> at its power
> and wonder.

One very practical and analytical woman told the story of experiencing God's grace after the death of her husband.

> I received a holy nudge. . . . I teach people not to give money on the street. . . . I saw a guy . . . with a thin blanket shivering. . . . I see this guy and he reminds me of my husband. And so, I walk up to him and said "Are you hungry"; he wanted a biscuit and coffee; I looked at him; in some ways he reminds me of my husband. . . . I am a sucker for blue eyes. . . . I had peace knowing that at least in part God put him there for me . . .

As she told the story, her voice conveyed the surprising, exceedingly delightful nature of this moment of a keen awareness of this existence after only knowing the pain of his absence before.

But the grace of God can be found in even the simplest of gifts. I remember visiting one church member who had practically lived in the hospital for months. My heart went out to him not just because of the illness but because as he spoke you could tell his life had become utterly bland and routine. He was not only sick but depressed by the monotony.

But in an instant, his countenance changed. His wife walked in with a "Sugar and Spice" pimento cheeseburger and fries. The tenor of the conversation changed and for a moment he forgot his misery and trajectory. A little kindness can become a heaping serving of the grace of God when given at the right moment.

But the place in which I have seen more joy over the gift of grace was at Trenton State Prison, a maximum security facility with 80 percent of those incarcerated serving maximum sentences for violent crimes. As a chaplain when I visited during the week, many of the men walked through the halls in a half state.

> They seemed almost comatose,
> but they were numb from the horror
> of the endless years
> of locked bars
> that faced them
> day after day,
> after day, after day,
> after day, after day . . .

> But when I visited on Sunday it was different.
> . . . Profoundly,
>   . . . incredibly,
>   . . . powerfully,
>   . . . wonderfully,
> different.

The first time I entered that chapel I felt like I had been transported to another world. and it was found in the music and the prayers. Music filled with the full measure of absolute freedom.

> Freedom from guilt.
> Freedom from feeling like something less than human.
> Freedom from feeling like a failure.
> Freedom from fear.
> Freedom in Christ,
> through the redemption in his blood,
> and resurrection from the tomb.

The scene was ripped straight from the Bible. They sang with a passion and joy completely unfettered by human expectations.

> Like that woman who washed Jesus' feet
> with her tears,

> so overwhelmed
> by the gracious love given to her.
> And as I watched that scene, I knew . . .
> I had never felt that kind of love for my Lord . . .
> . . . and then Jesus' words echoed in my heart, "Those who are forgiven much, love much."
> Now I knew in my head
> I had much to be forgiven for,
> but my sins
> hadn't broken the laws of society
> and led me to be locked up
> and discarded by the world . . .
>
> That was the only real difference
> between them and me
> in the eyes of God.

This leads us to Paul's opening words to the Philippians. Paul opened several of his letters with similar words because he wanted to set the stage for what would follow.

> As we know,
> Paul experienced the gift of grace
> in the most dramatic of fashions,
> when Christ struck him blind
> but did not strike him down.
> His deepest hope
> and the reason for his words
> was that others might know
> that grace as well;
> that they might know
> the freedom of those being released
> from the spiritual prison
> of their own making;
> that they might know
> in their hearts
> the greatest thing in all existence,
> God's loving grace and gracious love.
>
> So, with deep affection
> for his fellow Christians,
> he wrote,
> "Grace to you and peace from God our Father."

When Paul wrote these words, I am virtually certain he knew of the words of our Lord Jesus himself, "My peace I leave with you. My peace I give unto you. I do not give as the world gives." Remember Jesus said these words of grace right before Peter would deny him, the rest of his friends would abandon him, and one them would betray him to the cross.

> Indeed, Jesus does not give as the world gives.
> Our world is thrashing about
> with hatred, judgment, division, and fear,
> as seen in the social media frenzies, because it is deprived
> of the life-giving,
> joy-imparting,
> peace-bestowing
> breath of Christ,
> a supercharged,
> grace-filled
> love in our hearts.

And every Sunday we aim to fill ourselves up with grace so we can bring it to the world.

Some of you might wonder why each week in worship many congregations hit the pause button to greet one another. But that's not what they are doing in the passing of the peace. It is meant to be a moment utterly beyond politics, ethnicity, class, or religion; it is a moment when our hope for their life to be filled with the best things in this universe is conveyed in those few simple words.

In this moment we are sharing our yearning for our brothers and sisters that whatever is happening in their lives, be it illness, loss, confusion, weariness, apathy, sin, loneliness, that they might know the surprising grace through encountering the Peace of Christ,

> Each week in worship
> when we extend those words of peace to each other,
> we should look one another in the eye,
> while clasping their hand
> and opening our heart
> to its fullest measure,
> while considering the deep love God gave to us
> up on that cross,
> the profound peace of knowing Christ in our heart,
> and in the few words spoken,
> "The Peace of the Lord Jesus Christ be with you"
> offer it all to them.

How Can the Church Help People Experience God's Grace?

Church can be a place that either people flock to or flee from in times of loss. One person said something that might help keep people in the fold in these times.

> At times when I experience pain, church is the last place I want to experience God and not the place I want to be, as with death of my husband. . . . It is hard when you are single; it is hard to walk into the church. You will see a husband with his arm around his wife; people will not speak to you in any meaningful way. It just does not hit or resonate.
>
> I chose to change perspective; to change where I sit. . . . I went on the row with all the little old ladies, and one of them died and another left; that little support in worship left. Sitting with people in worship, the people I connect to, makes a difference.

Helping people know grace through the church in hard times often means finding people they can relate to and people that can relate to them.

The deeper challenge we face in helping people to experience God's grace in loss is that some simply do not. For them it is the dark night of the soul and the soul-crushing agony of deep loss. We must be careful not to heap on any shame or any more suffering or have a glib attitude if they have had no moments of grace. We must be clear it does not mean their faith is lacking.

And yet, it seems that teaching a resilient faith to begin with is important. We must not always send the message that God is Santa Claus showering us with goodies and presents all the time. At least this is how one woman explained it. She went on to tell the story of her oldest daughter.

> She was born with special needs. That night I was holding her, I remember that feeling, "What was happening?" And I felt a voice that was clear, "I will take care of her; it is going to be okay." Over the years it did not seem okay, but I always tried to do the right thing. However, whether teacher or school, wonderful people turned up in my life and, for twenty-four years, she was wonderful, chatty, and happy. . . .But little things cropped up. They did not know what it is, her kidney and heart. . . . She was diagnosed at twenty-four with a rare disease. . . . She died suddenly at twenty-five.

I could tell by the way she described the moment, even in her daughter's death, she found a moment of knowing God's grace. I was hesitant but desperate to understand and so I asked her to explain. "We never had to tell her there was nothing we could do for her; it gave me a lot of strength."

This woman's faith was exceptional, and I wanted to know more. I asked her to share with me that faith she grew up with and the faith she was taught. She described it as a resilient faith. From the beginning she was taught to expect that life would be hard and that, at times, God would demand almost more from us than we think we can give. She was taught of God's profound love in Christ, but also that God does most of the shaping and teaching of his disciples through trials. She said, "I learned so much from her. . . . I am committed to using my experience to help others. I feel committed to the idea. . . . What is the point if I don't use it for something good?"

Teaching a resilient faith, rooted in Scripture, is critical to helping people know God's grace in trials.

3

The Survey: Measuring Our Experience of God

AMID THESE HUNDREDS OF stories about the power and presence of God I wanted to gain a better understanding of which types of experiences made the most difference. I also wanted to know which general factors in a person's life, including their faith habits and relationships within and beyond the church, might influence this experience.

In consultation with members of First Presbyterian Church Spartanburg, focus group participants, and other clergy, I constructed a survey which was field tested and refined over a dozen times.

The survey includes forty-six variables divided into three categories: fourteen God-experience variables, fifteen church-related variables, and seventeen person-specific variables.

The God-experience variables focused on the power and frequency with which people experience God in nature, service, worship, music, hardship, and more.

The church-related variables asked the extent to which an individual has studied Scripture, how well they know their pastor, their perception of the church's involvement in justice and mission, and the strength of their personal church friendships.

The person-specific variables explored their theology, connections to family, a sense of purpose, generosity, whether they were reared in the church, and more.

The survey can be found in Appendix A and the full survey analysis is located in Appendix B. At this point all the results are drawn from First

Presbyterian Church in Spartanburg, South Carolina. In order to help you better understand the results, I will share a profile of the congregation.

It is an affluent, predominantly Anglo, 2300-member congregation in a traditional gothic stone building. It is very active and benefits from a culture in which church still matters to the daily lives of people. In 2014 the church experienced significant conflict centering on the denomination's change to allow same-gender marriage. Several hundred people left the congregation for a more conservative denomination. Those who remained, though still divided on the issue, were strengthened in their love for one another, their commitment to the church's mission, and their reliance upon the grace of our Lord Jesus Christ in all things.

As a result, we have over three hundred people every Wednesday night for fellowship, food, and learning. Circles are stilling going strong and eighty women come Tuesday mornings for Bible study. There are four strong children's choirs and the youth group regularly has over fifty students every week. The missions include supporting a meal ministry that feeds 1500 people every day and decades of overseas partnerships with churches in the Dominican Republic, Haiti, Cuba, and more. Recently, the church launched a Faith Initiative to End Child Poverty, gathering people from over seventy organizations and congregations to support those in deepest needs while working together to combat racism and policies that perpetuate the cycle of oppression. In short, First Presbyterian Church strongly benefits from a local culture in which Christendom remains strong, because it engenders deep engagement from a wide swath of members.

In order to draw broader conclusions, the survey will need to be conducted in other denominations and congregational settings. For example, the survey showed that liturgy was the least frequent and the least powerful place people experienced God in their lives. I would imagine this result would be very different in a Catholic or Episcopalian church.

Another question explored people's hungering for greater justice work in the congregation. It was relatively low for First Presbyterian, which is not surprising given the fact that the congregation also self-identified as predominantly conservative. The results could look very different, for example, in a predominantly progressive, African-American church in Chicago.

The first level of survey analysis rescaled all the answers to a range of 0–100. The survey began by assessing the frequency and power of people's experience of God in various parts of their lives.

GOD-EXPERIENCE SURVEY RESULTS

It was unsurprising that nature was the most powerful place in which people experience the presence of God (the mean answer was 80). All the focus group stories about nature came easily and joyfully. After all, it is the handiwork of the divine and to spend time in it is to literally immerse oneself into the canvas of our creator! More disheartening was the reality that the power of God in worship only rated 73 and the frequency of experiencing God there was even less, 71.

The lowest-rated item was not surprising, namely liturgy (Power 64, Frequency 63) I have long expected that Presbyterians have lost the thread of the true purpose of their liturgy and replaced it with themes, habit, and frankly disinterest! The most powerful place I have experienced liturgy, as you have gathered in the introduction, was an Episcopalian church! They have it figured out.

But of course, each tradition has its own challenges. Over a cup of coffee with my Episcopalian priest friend I shared our low rating on liturgy and my high esteem of theirs. He agreed with the sentiment but also said, "But the problem is some Episcopalians worship the liturgy!" Nevertheless, as a result of this survey First Presbyterian Church Spartanburg will be working on refining and honing our worship. Below are the full ordered results of the experience of God section.

Mean Self-Rating of God Experience on Power and Frequency Variables

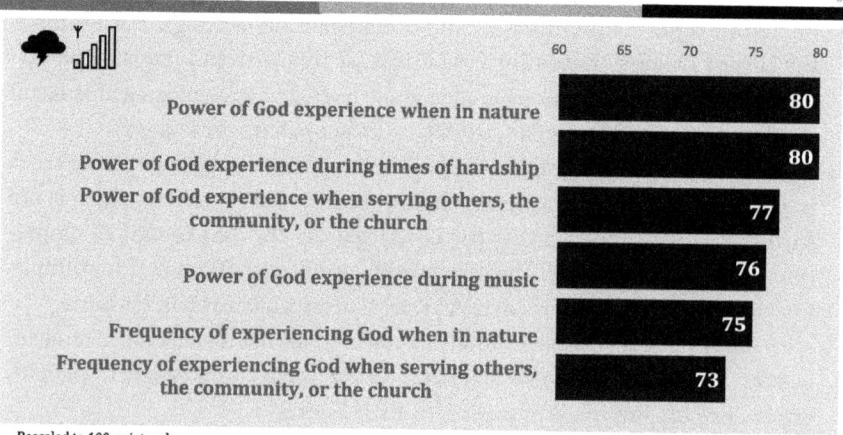

Rescaled to *100-point* scale

PERSON-SPECIFIC SURVEY RESULTS

It is important to note that the survey did not define any of the terms. Leaving the terms undefined enabled the survey to focus on the person's self-perception rather than comparing everyone against some established norm. In this way the survey taps into the person's existential identity. I wanted to tease out the individuals' core sense of self and how they measure up to their own expectations.

For example, in one of the questions on the person-specific section the respondent was asked to assess their generosity.

> On a scale of 1–6, 1 being very false and 6 being very true answer the following:
> I give generously of my finances

(In the rescaled analysis based on 100, an answer above 50 tended to be true and below 50 tended to be false.)

Note the question does not define generosity as a certain percentage of income. Each respondent defines that themselves against their own conscience. Biblically Paul tells us, "Each of you must give as you have made up your mind, not reluctantly or under compulsion, for God loves a cheerful giver" (2 Corinthians 9:7). Though religion is most often experienced within a community, it is lived person by person, and each person's internal self is ultimately only known to them and God. It is this self that our Lord is most interested in influencing as shown in the Corinthians passage. For this question the average response was 75. The highest-rated answer in the person specific section of the survey was 97, "I have someone in my life who loves me." Below are the full results of the Person Specific Results.

Mean Self-Ratings of God-Experience on Person-Specific Variables

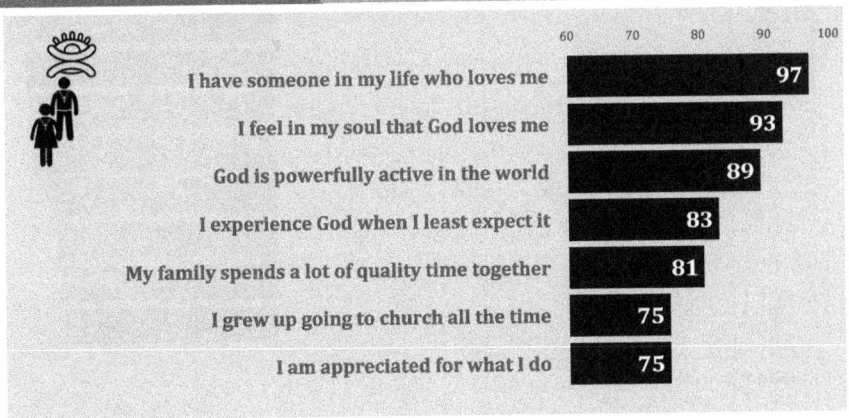

Rescaled to *100-point* scale

CHURCH-RELATED SURVEY RESULTS

The church-related section sought to glean their perception of the congregation. Given the extent of its mission work it was unsurprising that it was rated the highest at 90. Also, unsurprising but challenging was the relative lower-rated question, "My church is there for me in hard times." There are outstanding, loving, care-giving staff, as well as well trained and gifted Stephen's Ministers, but there still seem to be people falling through the cracks for one reason or another. This is a constant challenge in all congregations.

It was also good to confirm that there are many strong connections within the congregation as shown by the question "I have one or more good friends in the church" (84).

Another question asked the individual based on the same true/false scale to assess the following: "Our worship services are filled with hope and joy."

By not defining either the scale or the terms, the individual was forced to answer simply based on their internal scale. For this question the average response was 78.

Too often the modern world focuses on the external form of worship, for example whether it is contemporary or traditional, but the aim of worship is neither. Rather, it is to glorify the risen Lord. If the good news is being heard in word, song, and prayer then hope and joy within the hearts of worshipers is the inevitable outcome. This average response demonstrated that there is work to be done in the worship services. Below is an ordered list of the average responses for all the church related variables.

Mean Self-Rating of God-Experience on Church-Related Variables

Variable	Score
Our church is very active in mission	90
Our church music is excellent and inspiring	85
I have one or more good friends in my church	84
Our worship space helps me feel the presence of God	83
Our worship services are filled with hope and joy	78
Traditional worship is very important to me	77
I attend worship very regularly	76
My church is there for me in hard times	75

Rescaled to *100-point* scale

4

Going Deeper into the Data: What Drives Our Experience of God

THE TRUE POWER OF the survey was found in the next level of analysis. It enabled us to compare, for example, an individual's personal sense of generosity or the joy they find in worship to how frequently and powerfully they experience God overall in their life. The analysis assessed all the variables of the survey with this aim in mind.

The survey divided the respondents into four categories based on the power and frequency of their God experience overall in their lives.

- Type A: Often and Powerful
- Type B: Not Often and Powerful
- Type C: Often and Not Powerful
- Type D: Not Often and Not Powerful

The analysis showed

- 40% Type A,
- 12% Type B,
- 19% Type C,
- 29% Type D.

This was the (relatively) easy part. The true hope is to do what we can to move everyone toward Type A, which means understanding specifically which of the variables were most critical to becoming Type A, that is, to experiencing God frequently and powerfully. Of course, the complexity of the analysis was completely outside of my skill set.

I had just enough math in college to realize the survey presented a unique problem for the analysis. If you have around a half dozen variables it is not too terribly challenging to see which factors correlate with your objective. For example, if you want to know what is driving ice cream sales, you might examine several variables such as stock market fluctuation, gas prices, and the temperature outside. It may be that the stock market and gas prices have a minimal effect. But most likely outside temperature would be a strong driver—the higher the temperature, the higher the ice cream sales. But if you started adding dozens more variables such as the date, the wind speed, and geography, several of these factors would tend to move together (it tends to be colder and windier in January than August in South Carolina!) which makes it harder to isolate the key variables. With forty-six variables to sort through the task was daunting!

Thank the Lord for Dr. Jack Gallagher! He performed the analysis as well as offering invaluable assistance in constructing the survey. In his analysis he found the survey to be both reliable and valid according to statistical measures. He conducts medical research around the world, and using his considerable skills he identified five different variables as well as the percent to which they drive people toward greater power and frequency in their experience of God. In descending order of influence, they were:

1. The frequency of experiencing God in hardship
2. The power of experiencing God in hardship
3. An active personal devotional life
4. The frequency of experiencing God in worship
5. The power of experiencing God in worship

In the list below GE = God Experience. From Dr. Gallagher's analysis:

1. A member who "**experiences God most <u>frequently</u> during times of hardship**" was 3% more likely to be a GE Type A than were other members for each additional point higher on the questionnaire scale. The *relative influence* of this factor on member likelihood of being Type A was **29%**.
2. A member who "**experiences God most <u>powerfully</u> during times of hardship**" was 3.6% more likely to be a GE Type A than were other members for each additional point higher on the questionnaire scale. The *relative influence* of this factor on member likelihood of being Type A was **23%**.

3. A member who "**has an active, personal devotional life**" was 1.3% more likely to be a GE Type A than other members for each additional point higher on the questionnaire scale. The relative influence of this factor on member likelihood of being Type A was **19%**.
4. A member who "**experiences God most frequently by attending worship services**" was 2.3% more likely to be a GE Type A than were other members for each additional point higher on the questionnaire scale. The relative influence of this factor on member likelihood of being Type A was **16%**.
5. A member who "**experiences God most powerfully by attending worship services**" was 2.7% more likely to be a GE Type A than were other members for each additional point higher on the questionnaire scale. The relative influence of this factor on member likelihood of being Type A was **13%**.

EXPERIENCING GOD IN HARDSHIP

This means that experiencing God during times of hardship not only helps during the trials we face but profoundly impacts our experience of God at all times.

Of course, not everyone experiences God in hardship, and we don't want to create tragedy or loss to drive people to God. Unfortunately, though, the reality of life is that all people will experience hardship. No one is immune. These results show it is critical for the church to walk in compassion with people in hard times as well as to give them the tools to know God's presence.

In the focus groups, we heard many powerful stories of God's presence in hardship, and it was obvious those events continued to influence their experience of God at every moment.

I believe this can be attributed to the very nature of God. God is ever present and always with us. Jesus promised to send "the Holy Spirit, the Advocate."

First if the Holy Spirit is with us, then God is always right there to impact and change us. Unfortunately, our brokenness and sin have dulled our senses' ability to tune in to the divine frequency in our midst. When hardship forces us to turn to God it is like a holy adrenalin rush. It is like those stories of someone finding the strength to lift a car or run twenty miles to save another's life. In that moment the urgency of the situation awakens something that was always inside of them. That person moves through life now with a newfound sense of their strength and character. Hardship teaches our heart to tune to God within us.

Of course, not everyone is able to lift the car in an emergency nor does everyone experience God in times of deep distress. We must not make people feel guilty. Instead we need to seek to understand the key factors that make a difference.

One of those factors has to do with another of Jesus' promises, "Wherever two or three are gathered in my name, there I am in the midst of them." Think back to all the focus group stories. Time and again when people shared their experiences of God in hardship, they almost invariably included loving, generous, kind, and compassionate people at critical moments. In some way, Jesus' presence grows more palpable when people gather together. Jesus also promised us in Matthew 25 that we will see him in the face of others.

Next, consider, how hardship effects most us. Rather than seeking out the support of the community, we often withdraw from others. We don't want others to know that we have lost our job, that we are struggling financially, or that our marriage is falling apart. When a loved one dies, especially one of many decades, even coming to church can be too much to bear emotionally. However, Jesus' promise makes it clear that he can be found when we come together. The supreme and clear challenge we face as a church is to find a way to be an open presence precisely when people's instincts are to run and hide.

This requires an honest listening—listening to those who have not found the support of the community or the love of their faith friends in hardship. It means taking a hard look at the unintentional barriers we have erected that discourage people from seeking their faith friends.

AN ACTIVE PERSONAL DEVOTIONAL LIFE

Despite the importance of community there is another critical task the survey discloses for the church, both to help people experience God in hardship particularly and in life in general—cultivating a personal devotional life. After hardship this was the next most critical factor to move someone towards greater frequency and power in their experience of God, but the average response was unfortunately quite low (64).

It is not only interesting to note which factors were key influencers toward our experience of God, but which were not. For example, having studied the Bible extensively was not a key factor. Thus, simply knowing the stories or the analysis of the text does not on its own drive you to connect to

God. The intention of the heart in approaching the text was key. Practically every page of Scripture is overflowing with hardship and loss. In some ways, it is a book that tells the story of how people connect to God when life is extremely hard. This means that Scripture can serve as a road map to experience the presence of God. But it won't happen through osmosis. Instead, it comes through intentionally fostering within people clear, simple ways to learn to reach out to God in their daily lives. The focus group participants disclosed many various non-traditional means to do so. It does not always have to be a quiet, cloistered moment.

One man raced his bicycle through the forest with music blasting in his headphones but for him it was that time to also explore all the moments when God was active in his life. He would feel the wind in his face, see the beauty of God's creation while counting off in time with his heart beat all the blessings that God had given in his life. And it worked great for him! Personal devotional life does not have to mean quiet time, alone in stillness. But if it does for you than that is great!

There is another very simple practice the Catholics have engaged for centuries called *Examin*. It was described to me by a world-renowned Catholic educator at Boston College, Thomas Groome. He told us that at the end of every day either by himself or with his beloved, he reflects on those key moments in the last twenty-four hours in which he experienced the presence of God. In over fifty years, he said, "I have never found less than three." As I have tried this practice overtime not only do I discover that I experienced God's presence more than I had ever imagined but that I started to become more aware of it in the moment!

There are as many possible ways to experience God through a personal devotional life as there are individuals. The most important thing is not how you do it but to simply get started! Having said that, there are places and practices people have found most fruitful over the years and in a later chapter we will thoroughly explore how we might experience God through praying the Scriptures.

EXPERIENCING GOD IN WORSHIP

The third area of critical importance that drives us toward a greater power and experience of God is worship. It is important to note that neither knowing your pastor, having grown up in church, nor frequency of attendance on their own drove one's overall experience of God. Just showing up is not enough.

Even powerful and frequent experience of God in the music and/or the liturgy did not drive one's overall experience of God, nor did one's political leanings or theological beliefs influence one's experience. From this we can conclude there is something else happening within people's hearts than a surge of pleasure from the music or the chance to be with like-minded friends.

Each individual part of worship is critical but only when a part of a sound, authentic totality of an EVENT! This shows that coming to worship with an openness and a hunger for God are essential.

The openness to God is critical because God is the primary actor in worship. All we do in worship is in truth a response, but if our soul is deaf to God's Spirit whispering within us during that hour then it will be like speaking to someone on the phone whom we cannot hear.

Occasionally, when my wife, Wendy, and I are speaking on the phone she will accidentally mute the call with her face. She may still be talking but I cannot hear a word. At that point, I am only guessing that she is still on the line and I begin to utter random phrases (like "Wendy, I think your phone is on mute again! Wendy, Hello, I can't hear you!") in hopes that something is getting across. Sometimes this goes on for minutes because she may have not stopped talking! It is a very unsatisfying time as you can imagine. Without worship having the expectation and the space to hear God, it too will be unsatisfying. But there is a compounding factor. If we like the stories the preacher tells, or the mere sound of the music, we may enjoy worship and enjoy it tremendously but, without realizing it, still fail to hear the Lord!

NOT NATURE AND SERVICE?

A few key surprises were in the absence of certain drivers. Neither nature nor service were critical factors that drove one's overall experience of God even though nature was the strongest place people experienced God (80) and service was not far behind (73). It may be a result peculiar to First Presbyterian in Spartanburg, or it may be a factor of the small sample size, and yet, I still think the results are worth exploring.

Perhaps when service is construed as formal moments of volunteering without the critical component of worship or devotion people fail to connect it to God.

The less formal moments of being there for others always seems to engender a deep sense of the presence of God. Perhaps without the devotional moment of lifting it up to God it only serves as a momentary thrill rather than becoming embedded in the spiritual fabric of the soul. But perhaps there is something even deeper.

Part of the fundamental understanding of the Christian faith is that brokenness and sin are inextricable parts of the human condition . . . for every single person.

As Paul explained, none is righteous, not even one. Therefore, we all fully rely on the grace of God every moment, and humility is essential to a proper disposition of faith. Unfortunately, during material prosperity and health we may subconsciously delude ourselves that we are less in need than others.

This means, without realizing it, that when we help we may be doing so out of our own self-perceived largesse of time, money, or talent rather than being a good steward of the resources that ultimately belong to God. This is not to lay blame, for surely I am as guilty of this disposition as anyone.

This has critical implications for how we engage in service. It comes down to the difference between performing service for others as opposed to being on a journey with others. Lilla Watson, indigenous Australian artist and activist, once said, "If you have come here to help me, you are wasting your time. But if you have come because your liberation is bound up with mine, then let us work together." Service that works together in the name of God's love and grace for all will likely drive all of us to a deeper, more powerful experience of God.

Nature not being a key driver came as quite a shock. As we saw in earlier chapters it is a place of profound power. But perhaps its influence may be explained by the three key factors of worship, hardship, and devotional life. In fact, perhaps nature is the most powerful place to experience God because it easily conveys all three of these primary drivers.

As I explained earlier, when I hiked in the 100-degree heat of the Grand Canyon with a forty-pound pack I certainly knew hardship! But also, when I looked at the beauty of the ancient rock and considered the time, water, and pressure needed, I took a moment to contemplate what this implied about the fundamental nature of the divine and my relationship to the *mysterium tremendum* of God. In hearing the birds chirping, and the Colorado River rushing it became to me the sound of the voice of God which generated a sense of the glory and grandeur of God, which is the core of worship itself! So even though nature on its own is not a driver it remains perhaps the quintessential place to be!

5

A Practical Path to Experiencing God in Your Life

DRAWING NEAR TO GOD THROUGH PRAYER, THE BIBLE, AND VULNERABILITY

AT THIS POINT WE have learned a tremendous amount about other people's experience of God. Various factors such as Scripture, prayer, and vulnerability have been consistent threads that have strengthened experiences of God. We have discovered three key drivers for our experience: hardship, devotional life, and worship. In the next sections, I will offer a path to take that will combine these learnings so you can tune your heart to the Lord's frequency in your life.

First, we will examine several texts aligned with the types of God experiences drawn from the focus groups in chapter 1 that will allow you to study your stories in light of the biblical story. In the second part, we will explore several passages that you can immerse yourself in through prayer and a devotional approach to reading Scriptures.

COMPARING YOUR EXPERIENCE OF GOD'S HOLY PRESENCE WITH THE BIBLICAL STORY

Holy Presence

An ecstatic awe-filled surge of the powerful, mysterious, presence of God.

Theme Verse

"Come no closer! Remove the sandals from your feet, for the place on which you are standing is holy ground." (Exodus 3:5)

Take a moment to write down a time in which you experienced the presence of God . . .

Biblical example

Read Isaiah 6:1–8.
Isaiah experienced the raw unmediated presence of God. It is not sweet and gentle but filled with overwhelming power.
Some of the factors in Isaiah's experience:

1. The encounter was initiated by God
    a. Isaiah was not seeking God. Rather, God appears to Isaiah.
2. A profound sense of the glory of God
    a. With fantastic angels singing "Holy, Holy, Holy" and everything else within the scene, a wondrous sentiment is conveyed.
3. A deep overwhelming experience of the holiness of God
    a. Everything in this scene conveys the reality that God is something bigger and more fantastic than we can ever imagine. It underscores the infinite distance between God and humanity (i.e., the otherness of God).
4. An experience of the omniscience of God along with a sense of personal unworthiness

a. Isaiah is confronted by the frightening reality that God intimately and decisively knows his deepest, most intimate sin, which initially throws him into despair ("Woe is me!").
5. An experience of the omnipresence of God
   a. It only takes the hem of God's garment to fill the temple.
6. Worshipful
   a. Not only is it set in the temple, but there is heavenly song, confession, affirmation, and response.
7. Personal
   a. This event happens with Isaiah alone and in communion with the Lord and the divine servants.
8. Mercy
   a. The live coal cleanses Isaiah of sin, and therefore his guilt is removed, and he feels free.
9. Call
   a. This freedom compels him to want to serve the Lord. So he declares, "Here I am!"
10. Consider your own experience. What are some of the commonalities? What are some of the differences?

How might understanding this biblical event help you to identify those moments of God's presence in your life?

COMPARING YOUR EXPERIENCE OF HOLY COMMUNION WITH THE BIBLICAL STORY

Holy Communion

An experience of sacred, deep connection and a sense of profound unity with others on a level beyond kinship or friendship or the same experience in nature.

Theme Verse

All of you are one in Christ Jesus. (Galatians 3:28)

Take a moment to write down a time in which you experienced Holy Communion . . .

Biblical example

Read Acts 2.
   Factors of Holy Communion in Acts 2:

1. Gathered for a religious event
   a. People took time to come together for the purpose of worshiping with one another.
2. Gathered for an event of celebration and communal goodwill
   a. Pentecost was born as a celebration of thanksgiving for the harvest. The gathering was a time of joy for the whole community.
      i. "Rejoice during your festival, you and your sons and your daughters, your male and female slaves, as well as the Levites, the strangers, the orphans, and the widows resident in your towns." (Deuteronomy 16:14)
      ii. This event also came to be associated with the giving of the law at Sinai when Israel was shaped into the people of God!
3. Audible and visual stimuli add to the power of the event
   a. The sound of violent wind and the appearance of tongues of fire in this time of Holy Communion indicated that what was

happening here was not only in the hearts and minds of the people.
4. Deep understanding
    a. "Because each one heard them speaking in the native language of each." This event dissolved the traditional barrier and language and ethnicity and connected people based on their shared humanity. It is the miracle so hard to find in today's world when divided peoples truly understand one another and the barriers fall away.
5. Amazement and cynicism
    a. All were amazed at what was happening to them, the barriers were broken down, and the relationships were restored. But people scoffed at the community, believing they were intoxicated. Whenever God brings people together there are always those skeptical of the possibility who will forever doubt.

Consider your own experience. What are some of the commonalities? What are some of the differences?

How might understanding this biblical event help you to identify those moments of Holy Communion in your life?

COMPARING YOUR EXPERIENCE OF HOLY REVELATION WITH THE BIBLICAL STORY

Holy Revelation

An awakening to a deep truth with profound clarity; holy insight into God, life, and the world.

Theme Verse

"And you will know the truth and the truth will make you free." (John 8:32)

Write down a moment or event in which you experienced Holy Revelation; in which a truth impacted you in a powerful and unique way.

Biblical Example

Read Acts 10.
    Analysis of Acts 10:

1. Peter exhibits an openness
    a. Peter went up on the roof to pray, which means he was seeking God and was hoping to experience God.
2. God grants a vision and takes control of the encounter
    a. God responds to Peter with a divine agenda by putting Peter into a trance.
3. Peter's traditional faith resists
    a. "By no means, Lord; for I have never eaten anything that is profane or unclean." Peter bases his response on Scripture, so his resistance is unsurprising.
4. God draws in others through a providential encounter
    a. "Now while Peter was greatly puzzled about what to make of the vision that he had seen, suddenly the men sent by Cornelius appeared." God is asking something so radical of Peter, the change of a thousand years of tradition, that God will do more

to convince him and it will happen through connecting with others.
5. The vision has made Peter open to the encounter
    a. "You yourselves know that it is unlawful for a Jew to associate with or to visit a Gentile; but God has shown me that I should not call anyone profane or unclean." Before the vision Peter would have refused to meet with Cornelius. God used the vision to make him open to a great truth.
6. Sharing of God from the "other"
    a. "Four days ago at this very hour . . ." Cornelius speaks from the heart by sharing his own experience of God.
7. Holy Revelation
    a. This whole story culminates in a realization for Peter that is not only personally transformative but world-altering. "I truly understand that God shows no partiality, but in every nation anyone who fears him and does what is right is acceptable to him."

Consider your own experience. What are some of the commonalities? What are some of the differences?

How might understanding this biblical event help you to identify those moments of Holy Revelation in your life?

COMPARING YOUR EXPERIENCE OF HOLY LOVE WITH THE BIBLICAL STORY

Holy Love

A sense of unconditional acceptance by God, for others and for yourself, and a feeling of profound care and devotion.

Theme Verse

For God so loved the world . . . (John 3:16)

Write down a moment or event in which you experienced Holy Love through a sense of unconditional acceptance

Biblical Example

Read Luke 7:36–50.
    Analysis of the biblical story:

1. It took place around a meal / a time of fellowship (Luke 7:36)
    a. Meals offer a powerful time to connect. This is true across time and culture and shows it is something fundamental to the human condition. A meal can set the stage for deep sharing.
2. A lavish, bold, public action (Luke 7:37ff.)
    a. Great love or passion leads to actions beyond the norm. Often displays of love include emotional, cultural, and even physical risk.
3. To be loved leads to love
    a. This woman's experience of Jesus' love engendered a deep love for him in return.
4. Judgment and attempt to reassert cultural norms (Luke 7:39)
    a. Lavish love can lead to jealousy and fear, especially when it contravenes norms.
5. Bold acceptance over and against those in power and influence (Luke 7:40–43)

a. Jesus accepts this woman's actions despite the scoffing of those in greater power and position. He stands up for her actions, thereby reasserting control of the scene.
6. A lesson to be learned (Luke 7:44–47)
   a. Jesus uses this event to teach those present something about the nature of love. Those present despite their reticence have learned and been impacted by the event.
7. Words of acceptance (Luke 7:48, 50)
   a. Jesus publicly and unequivocally accepts the woman while also not pretending her actions of the past are not significant.

Consider your own experience. What are some of the commonalities? What are some of the differences?

How might understanding this biblical event help you to identify those moments of Holy Love in your life?

HOLY GIFTS, HOLY PURPOSE: EXPERIENCING GOD THROUGH A SENSE OF DIVINE PURPOSE IN YOUR LIFE GROWING FROM A SENSE OF USEFULNESS FOR GOD'S PLAN

Theme Verse

To each is given a manifestation of the Spirit for the common good.
(1 Corinthians 12:7)

Take some time to reflect on a time when God used your gifts to bless others and the world:

Biblical Passage

Read 1 Peter 4:10–11.
    Analysis:

1. Each has a gift
    a. The Bible makes it clear that God has blessed everyone with gifts. Often God uses unexpected gifts in those called to service.
2. Grace
    a. In one form or another all gifts are meant to disclose the grace of God. The gift discloses the inner nature of the one who gave it, grace and love.
3. Use the gift for divine purposes
    a. "Anyone who speaks should speak words from God." A divine gift by definition is very powerful. To use it for ill intent or personal profit is to subvert the will of God.
4. The gift is meant to glorify God
    a. "So that in everything God will be praised through Jesus Christ." God gives these gifts not so that we might be admired or thanked but to bring others to her/him in praise and thanksgiving.

Consider your own experience. What are some of the commonalities? What are some of the differences?

How might understanding this biblical event help you to identify those moments of using Holy Gifts in your life?

HOLY WORK . . . THE POWER AND PROVIDENCE OF GOD: AN EXPERIENCE OF GOD AT WORK IN THE WORLD; GOD'S PROVIDENTIAL POWER AND GOD'S HOLY TIMING

Theme Verse

We know that all things work together for good for those who love God, who are called according to his purpose. (Romans 8:28)

Take some time to reflect on a time when God's providence worked in your life:

Biblical Example of the Providence of God

Read Genesis 45:4–5.
Analysis (here we must analyze the Joseph story rather than these few verses):

1. Joseph's brothers act with their own intentions when they sell Joseph into slavery.
    a. Often our actions, even those with ill intent, wind up with very different outcomes than our own purposes.
2. Joseph rises to prominence in Potiphar's household and then falls. (Gen 39:20)
    a. Outcomes that initially seem very unfavorable through God's power can bring greater benefits. Quickly after being jailed, Joseph rises in prominence again. God can use any event for good or ill.
3. "God sent me before you to preserve your life"
    a. God used Joseph to bring about the divine will to preserve Israel through famine. Though Joseph was blessed in the process it was not for his own good but for his family's good.

Consider your own experience of the providence of God. What are some of the commonalities? What are some of the differences?

How might understanding this biblical event help you to identify those moments of God's providential work?

HOLY GRACE: EXPERIENCING GOD'S WONDROUS MERCY AND HEALING PRESENCE IN TIMES OF PERSONAL CRISIS, HARDSHIP, OR TRAGEDY

Take a moment to write down a time in which you experienced the grace of God . . .

Biblical Example

Read Mark 2:1–12.
   Analysis:

1. Some people bring their lame friend to Jesus looking for physical healing
   a. Moments of grace can often be spurred by good intentions even when they have nothing directly to do with the grace eventually given. They simply wanted their friend to be physically well. The key is coming to Jesus no matter our intentions. Jesus can always work with hearts led to him.
2. Jesus forgives the man of his sins
   a. The Lord offers this man more than he or his friends had even conceived of at this point—even more than they could appreciate at the time. Notice no one had asked for forgiveness but Jesus gave it regardless!
3. Jesus offers a sign
   a. Jesus realizes that grace cannot always be directly appreciated or understood. But so that the hearts and minds of all present could appreciate the gift of grace, he also gives the gift of healing. Note that the healing gift is in service to the greater gift of grace!

Consider your own experience of the grace of God. What are some of the commonalities? What are some of the differences?

How might understanding this biblical event help you to identify those moments of God's grace?

6

Experiencing God in Your Life through Praying the Scriptures

SINCE THE SURVEY SHOWED both that a personal devotional life is a critical driver to experiencing God and that many people are challenged by the very notion, the next section of this book will explore a time-honored devotional path to God using the Bible.

The Scriptures not only serve as a means to understand our own experiences of God, but the Bible can be the Holy Spirit's vehicle to connect us to the divine. Throughout the focus groups those who studied Scripture seemed to have a clearer grasp of God's actions in their lives. But the survey also demonstrated that those who had a regular devotional life had even more powerful experiences God and those who combined the two had the greatest results out of any profile!

Since Scripture was given to us by God there is an inherent power in it. The third-century theologian Origen described Scripture as sacrament. He believed that Christ was incarnate in the Scriptures and therefore could connect us to the higher wisdom of the divine. Add prayer to Scripture reading, and you have something very powerful indeed!

Prayer is central to the life of faith and the key means we have to connect to God. But like public speaking, many are intimidated by prayer, whether it is in public or in the privacy of their own mind. But not to worry.

There is a way for us all to grow into God through prayer no matter our facility and it has been performed by the faithful since the Psalms were first written thousands of years ago. It is called praying the Scriptures. If you have trouble knowing what to pray, simply reading the Scriptures with

EXPERIENCING GOD IN YOUR LIFE THROUGH PRAYING THE SCRIPTURES

a prayerful mindset is a profoundly simple . . . and powerful means to draw near to the heart of God.

In an ancient book on praying the Scriptures, *The Ladder of Monks*, a four-stage process is described that like the steps on a ladder raises us higher with each rung we ascend.[1] It culminates in the quiet stillness of the presence of God.

The quiet stillness of the presence of God!

Perhaps more than anything, I imagine many of you are grasping for something as sublime and beautiful as quiet stillness.

Through praying the Scripture such moments can be found anywhere! Even during gunfire . . .

Active shooters on college campuses have become a plague in our country. And in the fall of 2018 a campus had gone on lock down. Shots were fired and at 11:00 p.m. the alert went to the students' phones and they remained in place, turned out the lights, and listened for horror, terrified at what might happen.

More shots were reported, confusion abounded. One student called his father and they told each other about their love. The father checked the websites of the local news stations. They noted the active shooter status but nothing more. Over the next three hours they spoke briefly and texted. But not wanting to alert a possible shooter they kept their conversation to just a few words.

The young man's fear and dread continued to grow. The good news is the whole situation was confused and the students were never in danger.

But they did not know that.

The minutes turned to hours and each little noise magnified his worry. So, the son turned to what he knew. He turned to what his church and his parents taught him. He turned to what he learned in Sunday school as a little boy. It was simple but beyond powerful.

My son, Matthew, (my son!) closed his eyes, folded his hands, and said, "Our father who art in heaven, hallowed be they name . . ."

He recited the Lord's Prayer over, and over, and over again. And it gave him a measure of calm, some measure of peace.

Praying the Scriptures, specifically praying the Lord's Prayer, helped my son, Matthew, during a very traumatic experience. It turns out the Lord's Prayer is Matthew's go-to prayer. He has found he can use it for any occasion and any need. But this is hardly surprising when you think about it! It is the very prayer given to us by the Lord himself and of course it is part of Scripture.

Instead of the monastic path of *Lectio Divina*, I will examine four texts from the point of view of growing closer to God and then end each in prayer.

1. Guigo, *Ladder of Monks*.

Through learning how to pray the Scriptures we will discover that the presence of God is as close as the Bible on your bookshelf.

Specifically, we will see how we can . . .

- Draw near to God's glory through praying Psalm 103,

    Bless the Lord, O my soul,
    and all that is within me,
    bless his holy name.

- Draw near to God's strength through praying Isaiah 40:31,

    But those who wait for the Lord shall renew their strength, they shall mount up with wings like eagles, they shall run and not be weary, they shall walk and not faint.

- Draw near to God's love through praying 1 John 3:1,

    How great is the love the Father has lavished on us, that we should be called children of God!

- Draw near to God's grace through praying Philippians 4:6-7,

    Do not worry about anything, but in everything by prayer and supplication with thanksgiving let your requests be made known to God. And the peace of God, which surpasses all understanding, will guard your hearts and your minds in Christ Jesus.

Considering the importance of vulnerability, I will examine and pray these texts from my own story, which perhaps might help you to do the same.

DRAWING NEAR TO GOD'S GLORY THROUGH PRAYING THE SCRIPTURES

We will begin to learn how to pray the Scriptures in the Psalms. The Psalms are the Bible's prayer book, and as such any of them can be used for this practice. Specifically, we will explore how to pray Psalm 103:4-5. I first used these verses in my prayer life in seminary. Professor Jacks, who was a classmate of my father's at Princeton Seminary, taught us an ancient chant.

Bless the Lord O my soul.
and all that is within me Bless God's Holy name.

Bless the Lord O my soul . . .
and forget not all God's benefits
(Psalm 103:4–5)

The tune and the words have stayed with me even though it was twenty-five years ago! That is the power of praying (and singing!) the Scriptures.

We are turning to this text to learn how we can experience the glory of God. God's glory is hard to define but you know it when you see it. Perhaps most simply it is the beauty of the divine spirit, that which makes God lovely and wondrous which instinctively leads us to deep admiration and wonder.

This beauty of God of course is easy to see in nature. As Psalm 19 declares, "the heavens proclaim the Lord's endless glory!" My wife, Wendy, and I have accumulated six birdfeeders so that every morning we can see this glory. The hummingbirds are my favorite! To see the swift aerial maneuvers combined with their bright colors is amazing! They move so quickly it sometimes looks like a rainbow in flight!

The hummingbird is an astounding creature and so it shows us something of the inner Spirit, the character of God, just as a painting shows us something of the artist.

Our instinctive response to God's glory is to turn to God in blessings. So, let us now turn more deeply into the text to move us closer to God's glory.

The beginning of this verse is rather surprising. "Bless the Lord!" Blessing the Lord hardly seems possible. God is the one who blesses us, who gives us everything—our life, our breath, our food, our forgiveness, our hope. How then can we possibly bless God, specifically God's name?

It begins with proper respect and awe of the holiness of God. It's a respect lost to the modern world. So, to learn how, we turn to the chosen people. The Jews cultivate this awe through refusing to speak the divine name. Instead of "Yahweh" they say *HaShem*, which simply means "the name" in Hebrew.

The caution is founded upon the third commandment, "Thou shall not take the name of thy Lord in vain." The ancient Jewish rabbi Maimonides explains,

> Therefore if because of a slip of the tongue, one mentions [G-d's] name in vain, he should immediately hurry to praise, glorify and venerate it, so that it will not have been mentioned in vain . . .[2]

And no, he is not talking about swearing. Rather phrases like "God willing" or "God help us" that are often spoken without real thought of the divine. These through their lack of thoughtfulness diminish our respect.

---

2. Maimonides, *Mishneh Torah*, 12:11.

Thus, avoiding the use of the divine names keeps us ever aware of just how holy the Lord is—like not putting coffee cups on the communion table. There is nothing inherently sacrilegious about coffee cups. But treating the table like any piece of furniture can lead to a numbing of the specialness of the meal.

As we begin to grow proper reverence for the divine name a gradual deepening awareness of the holiness of God grows within us.

His name is utter perfection, utter purity. God's being is something so perfect and beyond us; this is the overwhelming part of the prayer; where we consider how finite we are in relation to this holiness; how fallen we are in relation to his perfection; how weak we are in relation to his infinite strength . . .

But for our lives to truly bless the Holy name of God our actions cannot be mere rote behaviors, like tossing some coin in the plate simply because it passes in front of us. The purpose of passing the plate in worship is not so much to get money to run the church (though we certainly appreciate it!) but rather to cultivate within us a disposition of deep thanksgiving and an offering of self to the Lord rather than a payment for membership in an organization.

In order to pray ourselves into this place we add the words "my soul." "Bless the Lord O my soul." It levels up our actions with deeper intent and more vital passion. When we put our soul into it, we are asking God to help us to be fully and thoroughly committed to the path of blessing God. Thus, we move into the words, "Bless the Lord, O my soul and . . . all (everything!) that is in me."

When you pray the Scriptures, you don't simply move directly through the text. You may hang onto a phrase and let it sink more deeply, or you might repeat it repeatedly. Through reciting this section multiple times, "all that is within me, all that is within me, everything that is in me, God!" your soul begins to connect to this concept; your soul resonates it in the repetition, like a singing bowl. The first few revolutions make little noise but in the continued motion they reinforce, and a glorious sound is heard.

That is what you are seeking when you pray the Scriptures. To resonate the divine in your heart.

As you say the words "all that is within me," you begin to examine yourself. With which part of my self am I not blessing God with? It leads you to ask God to show you these places in your life, to show you where you are holding back. (This is the place in which you become vulnerable before God.) Is it with my love of others? With my trust? Is it with my money? Is it with my body? Soon instead of wondering, the deep-prayer process leads you to clarity and a soul-felt yearning to wholly and utterly devote all that you are to God's glory.

Once we have grasped God's holiness and wonder we are ready to move into blessing God.

To bless God is to live the life God desires for us, to treasure what God treasures, and to care for that which God loves. Jesus so embodied this path that his life led people to see, believe, and glorify God. Jesus is the one who shows all of us how to bless God's holy name through our lives.

> Jesus had compassion for the poor, so to care for the poor is to bless God;
> Jesus was filled with forgiveness, so to be forgiving is to bless God;
> Jesus' heart was filled with love, so to love others is to bless God.

To bless the Lord is to live a beautiful life which leads people to give thanks to God.

Recently, I experienced this delight in a way I never quite realized was possible. In the summer of 2019, my family and I spent some time in Ocean City, New Jersey—a place my extended family has gone to for over eighty years. In fact, back in the day, my mother waited tables at a restaurant on the Boardwalk at Ocean City.

Ocean City does have a few advantages over the Carolina beaches, one of which is that it is not a stifling 100 degrees when you are sitting on the sand. But it does have its drawbacks, because sometimes even in June you need to wear a parka to walk along the shoreline!

So, I was walking along the beach with my daughter, Liz, my niece Johanna, and her new boyfriend, Matthew. As we were talking, we were having to raise our voices to hear each other over the wind and waves. Suddenly, we saw a beach ball rolling by. It was brightly colored and fun to watch as it picked up speed—going faster and faster and farther and farther—until it was almost a quarter mile down the beach.

Then Matthew turned around to see where this beach ball had come from. And we all turned our heads as well. We saw this young mother with her very young toddler slowly making their way to the beach ball. They were never going to reach it—it was getting farther away by the second. This young mother couldn't dash off after it; she couldn't leave her toddler.

When Matthew realized this, he took off after this beach ball in a full sprint and, after about a quarter of a mile, he reached it—right before it went into the ocean. He came back huffing and puffing and handed the ball to the mother. We all thought, "What a wonderful thing that he did."

But then, the mother turned and handed the ball to her young child. Suddenly, the child was hopping up and down. You would have thought he had won the lottery; he was giddy with delight; ecstatic! Filled with the most joy that only a child could have—it was unfiltered, giddy delight.

And I thought, "That's God." When we do those simple acts of kindness for others, it makes God giddy with delight. And that's how we can bless the Lord—make God just as joyous as a young child who, through an act of lovingkindness, was given back their beach ball!

With that, I will offer my own prayer on this text that perhaps might help you fashion your own.

Bless the Lord, Bless the Lord, Bless the Lord . . .

Lord I scarcely can know what it is to bless you.
You have showered upon me a life of great and exceeding joy.
Eyes to see the beauty of your creation;
ears to hear its wonders; and a heart to know the love of others.
You have blessed me with two wondrously made children
and a devoted, passionate wife.

You have called me to your service
and brought me to a congregation filled with life and challenge,
committed to a deeper walk with endless willing servants.

I cannot possibly begin to bless you, Lord.

Bless the Lord, O my soul . . .
O my soul, my soul;

move me God,
move my soul,
my innermost core of self
to yearn and hope for this with all my being. . . .
The very center of who I am,
move it to bless you . . .
may that which is within me point to your glory,
to you wonder
. . . O lord, O lord . . . Lord!

Bless the Lord O my soul,
and all that is within me bless God's holy name . . .

All within me . . .
all of it . . .
my mind,

my whole being,
my work, my words, my will,
my house, my family, my town,
my energy, my purpose,
my yearnings, my struggle,
my questions, my doubts . . .

may it all build to something greater
than my finite and feeble will,
so that somehow beyond reason
I might do something good for you God,
bless your name
through rising above my own meager intentions, efforts, and will . . .

Bless the Lord, O my soul and all that is within me, bless God's holy name. Amen.

DRAWING NEAR TO GOD'S STRENGTH THROUGH PRAYING THE SCRIPTURES

Next we will seek to experience the strength of God in our lives through Isaiah.

> but those who wait for the Lord shall renew their strength,
> they shall mount up with wings like eagles,
> they shall run and not be weary,
> they shall walk and not faint.
> (Isaiah 40:31)

This verse is a favorite of mine and many times in my life it has helped me draw near to the strength of God when my own strength was insufficient. It shows us the spiritual steps to draw upon the strength of God for any task that lays before us:

Wait . . . Launch . . . Soar

Wait for God's timing to reveal itself.
Launch your energies toward the goal to which God points you.
Soar on the winds of the Lord's will, letting the divine will take you all the way home.

"To wait upon the Lord" is the spiritual task of allowing God's timing to drive our life rather than our own anxious selves. Waiting is one of my greatest spiritual failings, perhaps seen most clearly in my inability to sit still through even one traffic light!

When we fail to wait, struggle and pain ensue.

As we seek the strength of God through Scripture, we will learn the wisdom of patience. For example, Jacob's stubborn, illicit actions cost him decades of his life, and Jonah's fearful fleeing endangered his life and that of others.

Waiting for God's strength comes from expectant patience in the life of faith, not from over anxious action . . . if we leap to action ahead of God we stray into paths that lack divine will and guidance, like hiking ahead of a seasoned guide can land you in a snake pit, or bear country, or unnecessarily rocky terrain.

I remember in Alabama feeling God call me back to the local church after serving five years in the presbytery. That was the clear, unequivocal calling. But I became restless and anxious. And in the waiting I let my ego allow me to be drawn to Atlanta to be the Executive Presbyter at the largest presbytery in the country. Now God used me there; so even in our mistakes God's power is still at work.

But there was no peace and my heart was still restless . . .

. . . Thank the Lord for Gloria and Lee Close who happened to attend a Sunday school class I was teaching in Atlanta which eventually led me back to the church as I answered the call to First Presbyterian Church of Spartanburg, South Carolina.

Ironically, in praying the Scriptures the most challenging effort is the waiting. This is the effort of quiet, of not trying to force insight and direction out of the text too quickly. It is staying in the silence of not hearing or feeling anything sometimes for hours or even for days in prayer.

Sometimes they are dry and unproductive. But I find that is the most important time to persevere because the payoff is magnified by the patience. This is true of sermon preparation as well. Sometimes when nothing comes to the preacher it is because God had something later in the week in mind for the sermon that does not happen until Friday . . . or heaven forbid even Saturday night!

To fully engage God's strength in your life means relying on God's timing, which enables us to launch with everything in our life properly aligned which leads us to step two in Drawing Near to God's Strength through Scripture—Launch.

Launching into God's strength is using all your energy toward God's goal. One of my favorite summer activities as a child was hopping on my bike and feeling the wind in my hair through the power in my feet.

I lived in Roanoke, Virginia, in the third through sixth grades and it was there my love for bike riding took off. I would ride my bike to and from school and to visit my friends. I would run errands for my mom and use it to deliver newspapers. The greatest days were on the weekends when my friends and I would meet at the 7-Eleven to play pinball games and drink cherry Slurpees! Those were the days! We would ride all day and if we were feeling strong, we would attempt the Challenge of Beer Bottle Hill! (Apparently the local teenagers gave it this name because it was shaped like a beer bottle!) The further up the hill you went the steeper it became!

The challenge was simple, ride your bike to the top without stopping. I had tried dozens of times. On a good day I could get to the neck of the bottle about two-thirds of the way up. But as soon as I hit that point my bike would begin to go backwards and I would have to jump off. It was extremely frustrating! More so because the older kids would see us attempting the challenge and would effortlessly ride to the top! It didn't even look like they were trying!

And that was the secret.

One day an actual teenager spoke to me and my friends and explained how he did it. "Even though it looks easy it isn't!" He said. "First of all, you are spending all your energy at the beginning, so you have nothing left in the tank when it gets hard. Pace yourself."

> Secondly you're all over the place! Be sure to drive with all your body into those peddles. Grip the bar firmly. Keep your knees in and not spread out especially at the neck when it gets really steep! Don't flail your arms, keep everything tucked in. That is what makes it look easy even when you are trying your hardest!

Within minutes we were all at the top of the hill! I think we made it to the top five times that day! But it took directing the strength of our hands, arms, and legs into those peddles with proper form—our whole body aligned and working towards our goal.

To mount up with wings of eagles in our spiritual life is to align our mind, our will, our heart, and our soul all to God's will for our lives.

Imagine God's will has become clear for your life but without spiritual alignment you will still flail and struggle; you will fail to gain God's strength. Even if you start in the right direction with your mind, if your heart is not in it you will fail to gain God's destiny for you. But in proper alignment through focused effort you can reach the top of Beer Bottle Hill invigorated by the effort rather than exhausted and move to the final and most glorious stage of them all!

Soaring! Soaring, on the effortless grace of the power of the Lord.

Once we got to the top of Beer Bottle Hill the fun began as gravity would take us racing wherever we wanted to go. We couldn't even peddle if we wanted to! Our feet could not move as fast as the hill was taking us! The wind whipping through our hair as we went faster and faster and faster with no effort was an incredible rush.

It . . . was . . . FUUUUUNNNNN!!!!!

Many birds look awkward on the ground, because God meant them to fly. Once they get airborne, they look at home, confident, and at ease. God meant us to fly on the winds of the Holy Spirit, for the Lord to be our strength.

Eagles don't constantly flap their wings, unlike hummingbirds; they cruise on vector currents that keep them aloft with little effort once they are on the winds.

Soaring is also like swinging on a swing set or bouncing on trampoline. The beginning takes effort but then your momentum perpetuates the process.

In praying the Scriptures at some point the perseverance pays off. And then the words pour forth in the rarefied air of God's wondrous love as one thought leads to the next and the next and the next.

It is all very good to talk about praying the Scriptures to draw us closer to God, but without practice it will come to naught. Praying the Scriptures is as easy as reading the Bible with a prayerful disposition. Let us bow our heads on our way into God's strength through Isaiah 40:31. It will be the words of the Bible in conversation with the stirrings of my heart.

Those who wait upon the Lord . . .

Oh Lord, let me wait,
let me have the patience, and the perseverance to let your timing be my timing.
Let me listen and watch for your signs to show me the way.
Even when it gets impossibly hard,
hold me back,
grab me by the neck,
and yank me back in your will and your ways.

. . . Wait, wait, wait and you shall renew . . .

Lord renew me within and without.
Renew my love for you.
Renew my hunger for your presence.
Renew my passion to follow wherever you lead.

Renew my courage and renew my hope.

. . . Those what wait upon the Lord shall renew their STRENGTH!

Lord my strength is all gone.
It is dried up.
I am weak.
There is nothing left.
I claim your promise
to invigorate my bones
and my flesh
and my soul
with the power of your Holy Spirit. . . .

God give me strength.
Strength to do your will.
Strength of character,
strength of the mind,
strength of the will,
strength of the body.
Lord give me strength to persevere.

Help all my efforts,
my whole soul and body and mind,
to launch as one into your will for my life.

Those who wait upon the Lord shall be renewed in their strength and they will mount up with wings of eagles . . .

With wings of eagles!
Lord give me those wings.
Lord be my wings.
Be my strength.
Let those wings release me from the burdens of my own making,
Lord please,
. . . Lord . . .

Oh, dearest and wondrous Lord.
Thank you.
Thank you for carrying me my whole life.

Carry me on the winds of your love and your grace.
Carry me and see me to the end.

> Let me soar!
> Soar in you,
> ... soar in hope,
> ... soar in purpose,
> ... soar in love,
> soar by your spirit
>
> ... Both now and forevermore. Amen.

DRAWING NEAR TO GOD'S LOVE THROUGH PRAYING THE SCRIPTURES

As the Bible tells us, "God is love," and since we are made in the divine image we are meant to be as well. In this section we will seek to align ourselves with the core of the divine character through experiencing this love in 1 John.

> How great is the love the Father has lavished on us, that we should be called children of God! (1 John 3:1)

I hope by this section perhaps you have attempted to pray the Scriptures. Like anything in this life, it takes some practice but, in this case, quick rewards will happen on even your first try. It's important to find a quiet place and still your mind. Try and give yourself at least ten minutes. It will feel awfully long at first. But it is important to get through the sometimes first few unproductive minutes.

I am a terrible runner. I have no stamina. Most of the time I start and stop every few hundred yards, especially at the beginning. But after about ten minutes it seems my body has finally realized I am going to subject it to this torment, and I find myself able to quicken my pace and even feel somewhat exhilarated by the process.

When you first begin to pray the Scriptures, you may not experience anything but a wandering mind, boredom, and emptiness. Don't worry! If you keep at it the Spirit will guide you to a place, as the hymn tells us, "Near to the Heart of God." You will find the mind of God who inspired the Scriptures to inspire your heart. It is about getting back to what the authors felt when they wrote the Scriptures to begin with.

Imagine that ... feeling what Paul felt when he wrote "faith, hope and love abide these three but the greatest of these is love," or the psalmist, what must he have endured and survived to confidently proclaim, "Yea though I walk through the valley of the shadow of death I will fear no evil!"

It is texts like these and 1 John 3:1 that light up my soul with the hope and wonder of the God who inspired such powerful words. When I pray this John text, it feels like I have entered his heart and the love he felt when he wrote these words.

John begins with the obvious, "How great is the love." We know it is great but to pray these words we should spend some to considering just how great it is.

Drawing near to God's love begins with the sense of the scope of the divine. Let this passage draw your mind to the notion that God's being is wider than the heavens, more intricate then the greatest fractal coastline, more powerful than the energy of a billion suns, more resplendent then the most beautiful sunset, more timeless than the most ancient of mountains, more wise then all the books in the world, faster than the speed of light, more inexorable then the biggest black hole; more thoughts than the fastest GHz computer with terabytes of RAM!

In both number and scope this greatness is even beyond the scale of that which we can appreciate it; just as a billion years is beyond our comprehension. Even though we know the number we cannot truly get a feel for it; we cannot even begin to get a true feel of God's greatness. But there are certain aspects we can appreciate. As Thomas Merton observed,

> Love seeks one thing only: the good of the one loved.[3]

Unlike human love, God's is utterly pure. God's love has no mixed motivations. God's love for us does not derive from some intrinsically endearing quality within humans, unlike our love. Often our love is like that for our pets. It grows for them when they give us pleasure through wagging tails, beautiful feathers, longing eyes, or endearingly obnoxious personalities. God's love for us is more like that for an amoeba which cannot give anything. It can only receive. Again, from Merton,

> Our job is to love others without stopping to inquire whether they are worthy. That is not our business, and, in fact, it is nobody's business. What we are asked to do is to love, and this love itself will render both ourselves and our neighbors worthy.[4]

God's love is absolutely unconditional. God loves the most hardened criminal exactly as much as the most giving saint. This is almost impossible for us to conceive. But as Paul wrote, "But God proves his love for us in that while we still were sinners Christ died for us" (Romans 5:8).

---

3. Merton, *No Man Is an Island*, 3.
4. Merton, *Letter to Dorothy Day*.

I loved our dog, Pippin, for sixteen long years, despite his obnoxious behavior, because he was endearingly ugly—both in shape and attitude. He had the legs and body of an Italian greyhound and the head of a chihuahua! And despite being only nine pounds, he would bark with the ninety-pound-Doberman-like ferocity at anybody he didn't like, and he didn't like anyone—except for Wendy!

He would growl at the mailman, at the neighborhood dog that was eight times his size, and at any male visitor! Sometimes this was annoying, but I really appreciated it when he would growl at most of my daughter's boyfriends. I was happy to see them not return!

When Pippin ran, his fast, cute legs would be a blur. And when he tried to turn a corner, he would slide like a cartoon character running in place.

When it was finally time to let go of Pippin . . . it was so hard. Wendy and I were with him—being blubbering idiots—I realized just how much I loved him. And I realized also that I didn't always love him as I should have. Perhaps I loved him less because he barked at visitors, ruined our carpets, and stole away the attention of Wendy.

But God's love is something that is always on full throttle; no part-way . . . no conditions, no provisional "if-then" nature. That is how great this love is.

But there is more to it and so John continues . . .

How great is the love . . . of the Father.

This means that God's love is personal and intimate. "Father" is not about God being male; God is neither male nor female but Spirit. Instead it describes the parental character of the Lord's love for us. Unlike other conceptions of the divine, Christianity's character is somewhat unique, and it is most clearly seen in our Lord Jesus with his disciples.

He shows them absolute commitment no matter how many times they fumble. He could have chosen to execute his task to save the world without them. But instead he drew near to this motley crew of no account and walked with them for three years sharing his heart and his life with them.

And so, we are a part of God's family. And no matter how obstinate and dim-witted we might be, Jesus will never leave us and will always draw us to his heart. And like any good parent his love is for our own best interest even when it hurts both him and us!

Jesus is willing to make his own life miserable in order to allow Peter to become everything that he was made to be. And believe me I am sure there were times when Peter wished that Jesus would simply leave him be. It is the love of a parent that will sacrifice everything for their child.

But there is still more. It gets even better. For not only is God's love like a parent but the good news it is also like a grandparent!

Many people have shared with me the joy of spoiling grandchildren. They give them ice cream and presents when it is not their birthday and generously and sometimes with reckless abandon let them know how special and loved they are. Which leads us to the next part of the verse,

> How great is the love of the Father . . . he has lavished upon us!

God's love is lavish, profligate, and prodigal.

Normally in Jesus' parable of the son and his father we think of the son as the prodigal one. This word means spending money freely with wasteful extravagance. Clearly the son fits this definition, but the father does even more. Not only does he give his son a third of his fortune just because he asks, but once the money is wasted, upon his return he throws a blowout party complete with a fatted calf!

That is about the most un-Presbyterian thing I have ever heard!

God lavishes this love upon us faulty humans, who keep soiling the carpet and barking madly and wildly at the cats of the world. God continues to love us who bite and bark at the hand that feeds us. This amazing God loves . . . us . . . loves me . . . loves you. Loves everyone with reckless abandon and will never be swayed from devotion, even when we do not deserve it. This is the great, lavish love of God our beloved parent who is always by our side.

I invite you now to listen in to my prayer with these verses, so they give you an idea of how to fashion your own.

> How great is the love.
> How great, how so very great,
> how so wondrously shockingly grand is the love you have, God.
> When I lift my head to the starry night sky, I see it.
> When I am refreshed by cool water, I feel it.
> When I am embraced by those who love me,
> it sends a wave of delight and peace up and down my spine.
> This love has been with me since the very beginning of my days and it has carried me in my darkest hours.
>
> When I have failed you,
> when I forget you,
> when I have turned from you,
> you remain steadfast and true, always steering me to my best destiny.
> Lord, you alone love me with a perfect love even when I am unlovable.

How great is the love . . . of the Father.

Of the Father, the Father!
God loves me like his very own child.
God, you are immense and immortal.
You are omniscient and the greatest thing in all existence.

And yet, you choose to call me your child.
You choose to welcome me into divine circle of love!
Bless you, Lord, for this supreme gift beyond my wildest hopes.

How great is the love the Father . . . has lavished upon us!
Lavished, lavished, lavished?!
How can this be, O Lord . . .

Your love, O Lord, is not calculated or measured,
it has no accounting or conditions,
it has no throttle or brake,
but pours out like a waterfall in spring,
dousing us with divine delight!

"*Thanks be to God for this indescribable gift!*"
Amen.

DRAWING NEAR TO GOD'S GRACE THROUGH PRAYING THE SCRIPTURES

> Do not worry about anything, but in everything by prayer and supplication with thanksgiving let your requests be made known to God. And the peace of God, which surpasses all understanding, will guard your hearts and your minds in Christ Jesus. (Philippians 4:6–7)

Grace is often described as the unmerited favor of God, especially when it comes to our salvation through Jesus Christ. But, in fact, it applies to all those moments in which we receive a blessing from God unexpectedly in the most surprising of ways. It is a gift from God, and it is so great because like receiving a present when its not our birthday it comes out of the blue, knocking us sideways with the love and kindness it shows.

Let's face it, we are all in need of grace, sometimes desperately so. It is not because times are worse. Not by a long shot. In fact, *The Atlantic* reported that 2015 was the best year in history for the average human being![5] But even though we are better off than ever before, life is increasingly complex. And even though it is better for humanity, there are still many good reasons to be anxious. There always will be, no matter the phase of life we find ourselves in.

Those in the "sandwiched" generation find ourselves worrying about our kids and our parents. Those of younger years are trying to find the balance amongst career and family and a sense of purpose. Those in the latter years of life are trying to stay healthy in body, mind, spirit, and finances to be able to age in place. These are all good reasons to worry.

The apostle Paul had a lot to worry about. His life was constantly being threatened and many times he lost the support of his fellow Christians. But shockingly he writes these words from Philippians,

Do not worry about anything.

Can you imagine? No worrying . . . about anything?! It not only seems impossible, but wholly unreasonable given the challenges in our lives. But here is what I think he meant.

One of the great blessings of serving First Presbyterian Church of Spartanburg, South Carolina, is the staff and the church members. I once heard David Renwick, the previous pastor, say that there are more leaders at any meeting at First Presbyterian than in entire congregations he has served! And he is right.

In January of 2019, when I was going on sabbatical the timing meant I would be absent for almost all the planning for a major summit on poverty that our church had initiated. But I was not worried. I was not anxious (okay I was a little anxious), because I knew those in charge were far more capable than me in making this a successful event.

Not too long after the conclusion of the summit, I heard that David Dodson, our consultant, who works across the country, said that ours was the single best event he had ever seen. Ever!

So even though the event was complex and had many pitfalls to avoid, I knew it would be successful because I knew the people who were planning it. Paul is not trying to tell us there is no reason to worry. Rather he is telling us to give it to God, the most capable, conscientious, and wise being in all existence.

We need not worry about ANYTHING. Don't worry because God says to us, "I got this one." . . . And Paul tells us how to hand it off to God. To let go of it.

Prayer.

5. Kenny, "The Best Year."

But in everything by prayer and supplication . . .

It is through prayer that we hand our worries to God. Furthermore, it is through the amazing grace of God that often in the most unlikely of moments we receive the healing we hoped for, the job we were seeking, the friendship restored, or even the blessing of a peaceful letting go of a loved one after a long illness.

I am so thankful for all the participants in the focus groups who shared their experiences of God. They have blessed me tremendously.

Many cited moments of prayer that brought grace. Their examples show us all that prayer works.

Sometimes what we truly need is not so much for God to fix things but to ease our heart. I know I spent hard, sleepless nights when Liz went to her first day of school, her first sleep over camp, her first date, and her first day of college. Basically, all the firsts! What I needed was to chill! I trusted Liz and the people who were caring for her. But I simply couldn't help but worry.

One person shared what happened when she took her worry to God, while praying over a child leaving the country to do mission work . . .

> He enveloped me in his peace. . . . I cried tears of joy! Sometimes God surprises us in prayer and in the blink of a moment we can move from fear, worry, and anxiety to tears of joy!

Other times grace may come after months or even years of waiting. Perhaps you have been seeking a new direction for your life. Maybe you have felt it is time to move or change jobs. There is all this waiting, all this worry about what to do and you're not sure how in the world you're going to make this decision and then one day completely unexpectedly God's gracious surprise is clarity.

This was the experience one person shared. They came to a church event not even thinking about the decision they faced when suddenly everything in the event seemed to point to God's will for her life and so she wrote,

> I took a walk and prayed for 30 minutes. . . . My head exploded with thoughts that were not my own. It was deeply moving. . . . I felt so clearly God was helping me. Filling my mind with clear messages that were unlike anything I had experienced before.

She hadn't come to church thinking her future path would unfold but through God's surprising grace it came.

Sometimes God's grace comes even when God says no. We have all found ourselves praying for healing for a friend or loved one. We have seen them suffer greatly and seeing our loved ones in pain is agony. This is what one person shared,

> I had a dying friend that I tried to help in the last stages of her life. There was pain and suffering and praying and pleading. God came through for us. She passed away but did so with no pain. It was amazing.

Even though it was a moment of loss, there was grace. Because in the respite, in the release through prayer God gave her a sense of assurance, that release from this earthly coil of pain and sickness was a moving on from this life into glory in the next.

. . . And the peace of God, which surpasses all understanding, will guard your hearts and your minds in Christ Jesus.

God's gracious acts of love are so surprising because they grant us a moment of peace when we least expect it. We can't understand it because it comes beyond expectation. In the midst of pain, parental worry, and personal life trajectory these people found God's peace beyond all reason because prayer works.

So, believe it! Above all reasonable expectation God wants your prayers. Despite being very busy God grants us a willing and listening ear. God wants me and you to hand over our small problems and our big ones.

What better gift for your life than the power to not worry . . . about anything! That is the power of praying this text from Philippians.

I invite you once again to listen in to my prayer on this text, that it perhaps might cajole your imagination to prayer in your own way through this text.

> *Do not worry,*
> God are you serious?!
> I have a new house!
> Two houses now, since the first has not sold!
> I am going away on Tuesday for a month.
> Backpacking in the wilderness.
> It will be amazing,
> but I have not done this for thirty years.
> My itinerary is not set yet.
> Do I have all the gear I need?
> My father has moved in with his fiancé.
> His memory continues to fail.
> Will it work out?
> The poverty initiative is gaining momentum.
> Can I leave it?

I love Spartanburg,
but how can it be that two different worlds exist
in the same town?
With seventeen years' difference of life expectancy
from Converse Heights to the Northside?
Help us to not only talk the talk
but walk the walk,
joining hands with all our brothers and sisters,
to make this town and this world
into your vision of justice, peace, and love.
Lord there is so much to be done . . .

    Don't worry Tom . . . about anything.
    Keep working. Keep failing.
    You have seen my blessings all your life.
    You have read about them in my word.
    You know you can trust me.
    Let go.
    Let go of your worry.

But in everything in prayer and supplication . . .

Lord, give me the words to pray.
Give me the heart to pray
your hopes and dreams for this world.
May your Spirit
so fill my soul
that what pours out is your will.

And the peace of God which passes all understanding,

Lord, give me that peace.
Lord, give that peace to our world.
Lord, confound us with your grace.
Let your grace surprise me,
let it surprise us all.
Shows me the face of Jesus
in everyone I meet,
this day, and every one that follows it.
Amen.

7

Experiencing God through Worship

MAKING WORSHIP WORK

IN THIS CHAPTER WE will be exploring a few key parts of worship to enable us to praise God with greater joy, offer ourselves with more fervent hearts, and pray to God with deeper reverence. In the interviews it became clear that there are certain parts of worship that a lot of people have a harder time connecting to mostly because there is not a full understanding of it, nor how all the parts form a unified whole. Since, as the Westminster Confession teaches us, we were made to worship God and enjoy God forever, it would behoove us to grow in our ability to do so with everything we have: body, mind, and spirit. Hopefully by the end of this chapter you will not only know more but be better able to bring your whole self to this sacred time.

THE OPENING AND THE CALL TO WORSHIP

Our worship begins the moment we walk through the narthex doors. Psalm 100 tell us to enter those proverbial gates with thanksgiving because entering God's house is a profound moment in our week. It is focused time with our brothers and sisters in Christ to offer ourselves in praise to our Maker.

But I imagine such focused hearts elude most of us. We come rushing from Sunday school trying to find our pew and our friends. We come having wrestled with our little ones trying to get their Sunday best on or having to roust our teenagers out of bed. Perhaps our Saturday night bled into the early hours of Sunday morning and we simply feel lucky to get to worship.

Whatever the circumstances there are many reasons we are not so focused the moment we enter. I am certainly as bad as anyone. I am thinking about my sermon, whether the acolyte's fire will go out, whether the guest speakers have been properly instructed; the sound system, the flow of worship, and on and on and on—wanting each part to fuse into a unified whole for us all to properly honor our Lord.

The secret to a better beginning in worship is to prepare before you even arrive, when you wake up in fact. As you wake on this day, you should begin by remembering, this first day of the week has special significance for Christians. Scripture tells us Jesus rose on Sunday, and early Christians referred to Sunday as the "Lord's Day" (Revelation 1:10). The significance was so deep for Christ's followers that they moved their worship day from Saturday to Sunday.

As you approach the sanctuary your heart and mind should be experiencing what some have called a "little Easter" every week: a deep sense of thanksgiving and joy for God's resurrecting and reconciling power made possible through our Lord Jesus Christ.

In fact, in the early church, Sunday, as the day of resurrection, was considered to be the "eighth day of creation"! Every week as we celebrate Christ's resurrection, we should enter worship with the expectation God will create something new and powerful in our hearts, minds, and lives.

Whatever distractions we entered with are meant to be purged during the prelude. The contemplative music, its beauty, and structure are meant to lead our soul into the presence of God. It should be a time of prayer and asking for God's Spirit to make you fully present this hour. A sense of expectation and energy should build as we approach the Call to Worship. It is our first overt act together and as such should serve to create and express our collective praise.

It should be drawn from Scripture as it extols the central aspects of our Lord—God's glory, love, honor, might, steadfastness, and mercy. It should be about God and not us, taking us beyond self-concern to focus on a praise worthy of our Lord. It should remind us worship is about what we offer to God in thanksgiving not about our personal wants and desires from this hour.

Psalm 100 is the prototype for the Call to Worship, with each piece building our praise, "Make a joyful noise!" prompts us to exude energy and delight.

"All the earth" reminds us that we are joining all creation in this act of praise. As Isaiah declares, even the trees of the fields will clap their hands! It joins us into a powerful sense of an earth-wide praise growing our connection to all the people, especially all our brothers and sisters in Christ.

In challenging us to "know that the Lord is God," we realize worship is fundamentally an act of acknowledging the "godness" of God. Worship only belongs to the Lord, meaning only God deserves our eternal praise. The Psalm expands on this theme by reminding us, "It is he that made us, and we are his."

In this moment we realize our longing for autonomy and freedom is in fact a distortion of our idolatrous ways. In acknowledging "it is he that made us," we joyfully admit that we are not even lord of our own lives.

At first this might be troubling, but the next phrase reassures us, "We are ... the sheep of his pasture." Yes, our lives don't belong to us but thankfully they belong to a nurturing shepherd God who watches over us and disciplines us with love.

Having called ourselves together and then praised the Lord in song we are ready.

THE CONFESSION

> We are to confess and to truly mean it.
> We are ready for God to do something to us;
> we need God to do something for us;
> for our praise is imperfect,
> and our hearts have divided loyalties.
> So even this moment of confession is not about us,
> but about making our praise of God pure and more authentic.
>
> But the refining fire is no picnic;
> it burns ...
> but it is a burn that eliminates
> the deadwood in the forest,
> for if we let too much accumulate in our hearts
> it can be a fire that burns us up,
> if we don't clean out our soul detritus each week.

Psalm 51 serves as our prototype for confession. When it declares that "my sin is ever before me," it reminds us that each week there are many things that have created a barrier between us and God. And just as you might move to the other side of the street when you see someone you owe money to, we avoid God when we are in debt.

Think about those people you have wronged. It creates an awkwardness when you see them, doesn't it? That tightness in your chest is joined by a fear in your mind that somehow you will be called out, shamed, and shunned. If the offense is not resolved there will always be a barrier between your heart and theirs, like that relative you have avoided for so long. I imagine just bringing that person to mind right now makes your heart beat faster and your breath get shallower.

But that relationship will never be fixed unless you have the courage to reconcile.

So, the next phrase from the Psalm, "Against you, you alone, have I sinned," reminds us that every act against a stranger, neighbor, or family member is, first, an act against God. That phrase enables us to see the truth of our sin.

> It means there is a part of us
> that as we go to God in confession
> should be filled with a holy terror,
> for we know there are many, many times
> we have sinned through our thoughts,
> words, and deeds,
> by what we have done,
> or what we left undone.
> We remember that God is a Holy God
> who abhors sin,
> who will not tolerate its presence.
> Dozens of times the Old Testament asks
> in one form or another,
> "Who can stand when you appear?"
> "Who can abide the day of his coming?"
> We remember that God's divine wrath burns hot,
> when we do not use our power
> to help those in deepest need,
> when we covet our neighbor's blessings,
> and when we seek our own justice for minor needs
> but neglect to work it for others
> who have been profoundly wronged.

During this time in worship we must fully realize the shocking, dangerous nature of our sins for it to be effective. For only the fullness of our sorrow can lead to an authentic soul-felt desire to reach out to God through asking, "Have mercy on me, O God, according to your steadfast love."

We ask God for this mercy not presuming it will come again even though we have already received seventy times seven and more. We know

God is not obligated to forgive. It comes to us as an unmerited gift. We do not presume. We are almost as tired of our sins as God is. So along with the psalmist we pray,

> Create in me a clean heart,
> O God,
> and put a new and right spirit within me.

We realize in this confession time that our ability to be free from sins depends upon God's power not our own will. Sin is a power of which no mortal has control, so we ask God to fix it for us;

> create in me,
> put a spirit in me.
> PLEASE!!!

As Luther so powerfully penned in "A Mighty Fortress is Our God," "on earth is not his equal." We cannot stand against the power of sin except by God's power.

This means surrendering our will to the Lord's and welcoming the Spirit's power in our lives. But if we don't truly recognize our sin, we won't truly invite God in. But if we truly confess our sins as 1 John admonishes us to, God will cleanse us of all unrighteousness.

Imagine the promise in that. We are tired of making the same mistakes and living with the same fears, but in surrendering to God we truly can become something new.

THE ASSURANCE

Once we have truly felt the depth of our sin in that confession and experienced the sheer, holy wrath of our God and been in mortal terror, if only for the briefest of moments, only then are we ready to hear, understand, and believe the Truth of this Incredible God.

Our God is a God of infinite mercy and love.

> For as much fear we knew
> for the briefest of moments,
> we shall know an infinitely greater,
> sublime,
> rapturous,
> resplendent,
> and refulgent
> JOY!!!!

In the Assurance of Pardon, we see, hear, and feel those cleansing waters of Christ's supreme grace. We truly are ready to accept that God forgives and forgets. God wants us to confess so that we might know the divine mercy and believe.

> To believe,
> that as Psalm 51 tells us,
> "wash me, and I shall be whiter than snow."

Our sin is not like that ketchup stain on your white polo shirt. Yes, you washed it and it mostly came out. But you can still see it and you know no matter how much you scrub it there is always a reminder of your clumsy eating habits (a lot like all my ties!).

But God scrubs us so thoroughly from sin that we are whiter than snow. We have been cleansed with such power that there is no microscopic residue left. It is GONE!

Having offered God praise, confessed our sin, and been assured of God's mercy, now we are ready to hear the good news with an eye to actually becoming what God has created us to be.

THE WORD AND THE SERMON

The word of God has power for life. Real, palpable, transformative power. It is a power that works for any person in any stage of life. Some months ago, I challenged the children to memorize Psalm 100. Several of them came to me and recited that marvelous passage. And as each recited it, I could see in their faces and hear in their voices that they knew something special had been placed in their heart through their hard work.

You can take Scripture to work to give you the courage to be honest by remembering, "Let no evil talk come out of your mouth but only what is useful for building up."

. . . You can call to mind Paul's words when all threatens to fall apart, "Do not be anxious about anything but in everything let your prayers be made known to God."

. . . And when you are feeling worthless you can remember the Psalms, "I am fearfully and wonderfully made."

Every time is the right time to call to mind the word of God. But especially Sunday mornings!

The reading of the word is paramount to any worship service for it is inspired by God. In 1 Timothy Paul uses a very rare word to describe

God's word, *theopneustos*, which literally means God-breathed. (By the way "inspired" comes from the Latin *inspirare*, meaning "breathed into.")

This means we believe God's Holy Spirit uniquely illuminated the Biblical writers to convey God's truth, so it serves as a guide for life. As Psalm 119 tells us, "Thy word is a lamp unto my feet and a light unto my path," so we read it in the common language of the people, for how can we be guided by it if we don't understand it?

Although it was written long ago, through God's continuing presence of the Spirit it speaks to us now, guiding, comforting, and convicting. Before the Scripture is read, we have a prayer for illumination (sung or spoken) so that we might be ready to hear the Spirit's power. Your heart and mind should be racing with expectation as you approach the word, for something amazing is about to happen!

As the *Book of Common Worship* explains, "The God who speaks in scripture speaks to us now."[1] God is speaking right now, in this place, at this time!

We must read Scripture in worship because we come to hear God speak to us first and foremost, not the preacher! Your inspiration in this hour should not rely on the charismatic power of the preacher (or lack thereof!). The preacher's task is to illuminate the word, not to share their own personal wisdom.

The Scripture is the unique authoritative witness to God. But it is not a power intrinsic to the text on the page, but always tied to the Spirit who inspired it. This means we don't venerate the text or treat it like the fourth member of the Trinity. In the end it is a book, not divine. Any other thought is idolatry.

Such idolatry led to the martyrdom of several heroes of the faith. The church refused to allow it to be translated into the common language of the people, so William Tyndale, the translator who, according to church historian Martin Marty, more than anyone gave us the King James Version of the Bible, was burned at the stake in 1536.[2] Because of past abuses we emphasize an important distinction.

Presbyterians believe there is a difference between inspired and dictated. In the Mormon faith it is believed the Book of Mormon was found on golden plates by Joseph Smith. Furthermore, it is believed that through a special stone he was able to absolutely without error translate it into English, a perfect copy. In the Muslim faith it is believed the angel Gabriel dictated the Koran to Mohammed, word for word.

---

1. *Book of Common Worship*, 37.
2. Marty, "Believers Babble over Bible."

Presbyterians believe that God inspired the authors, but like any inspiration the character and personality of the authors emerged as well. Take Monet's *Water Lilies* for example. To stand before it is to feel and see something incredible. Something God created but also something Monet created. The dazzling colors, the light and shadow, and the verdant, abundant vegetation exudes supreme beauty and peace, but it is not nature itself but a painting. Clearly, some of Monet is on that canvas.

When we read Paul's letter clearly his own perspective and insights come through. He even tells us as much, "I see in a mirror dimly!" And like Monet's painting, this is a good thing, because it invites us to realize we too have a perspective and insight.

This is one of the reasons we not only read the word but preach it as well. We interpret the author's context to unveil its power today.

I know that you have read a certain text in the Bible and found no insight, comfort, or direction. For me it was Deuteronomy. I just didn't get it. It seemed only to contain meaning for the Israelites from thousands of years ago that were emerging from the wilderness into the promised land, with no meaning for us today. But then a preacher unfolded its power through a dance of explication, archeology, Hebrew language research, and his own personal love for the text. Suddenly, that text now sings and speaks to me as the Spirit's inspiration leaped from the biblical author, to the preacher, and now to me! In some way the task of the preacher is to bring people back to the point that inspired the biblical author to begin with.

But the preacher also needs to be careful.

Since the authors of the Bible inevitably shared some of themselves sometimes the authors' own preconceptions come through. Failure to realize this bias has justified some of the worst abuse across history such as slavery, genocide, and the subjugation of women along with leading to scientific illiteracy! These are horrors created by lazy interpretation and self-serving societies, so the preacher must take the context and history into account.

As J. Christian Beker, a professor of mine at Princeton Seminary, explained, our task is to find the abiding, enduring word of God amid the contingent word of the time in which it was written. The Bible offers us so much. In getting to hear it each week is the chance to hear the wisest, most pertinent, trustworthy source in all the world. But it needs to be preached because much of it comes to us through a culture, a language, and a people.

At first you may feel this diminishes its power. But in my own personal experience, this realization has amplified it by opening critical insights.

Take for example the creation story in the first chapters of Genesis. Early in my life I simply took it at face value. Then as I learned more about geology and biology, I began to ignore those early chapters. But when J. C.

Beker convinced me in seminary that the Spirit still speaks uniquely and powerfully through those texts, I hit the books. And I saw what he meant!

Those chapters in Genesis were written in a time and culture when the people surrounding the Jews believed in an evil god named Tiamat. This evil god was slain, and her drops of blood became humans and from her carcass was fashioned the heavens.

So even though I don't go to Genesis to learn science, there are still fundamental truths to be found there. Against the prevailing views at the time the Bible was written, Genesis teaches that the world was created by Yahweh, not the carcass of an evil god. And that people are made in God's glorious image, not form evil blood droppings!

Ultimately though we don't read and proclaim the Bible in worship to learn how to be better people or even to understand the faith more clearly but to have an encounter with the living Lord. We don't come to so much learn truths about God, but to meet God in Jesus Christ.

The true purpose of preaching is to illumine our minds in order to ignite our hearts in holy love for Christ.

It is that moment in the sermon when the preacher before you dissolves away and suddenly it is the Christ you feel, right there with you. When the word of God leaps off the page and comes to life. It happened for me in 1994 in the first few months of my ministry.

I was visiting my grandfather in the last days of his life. For the first time I saw him look vulnerable as he lay prostrate in bed. The six-two, 220-pound man had shrunk down to skin and bones of 140 pounds. I searched for something to say. "Grandpa, do you remember that home on Snowden Lane with the creek that we went fishing in?" No response. I tried again. "Grandpa, how about that soup grandma made, oh it was so good?"

But nothing registered and he looked so helpless. Since my childhood my grandfather had represented stateliness and power. I never saw him without a tie the first twenty-five years of my life. I had given up and begun to leave. And remembered one more thing. A few weeks before I had conducted a funeral service. I said more to myself than to him: "Grandpa, I conducted a funeral and used Romans 8." As I was turning to leave, I heard a barely imperceptible voice,

> "The sufferings of the present time will not compare to the glory about to be revealed to us." Tom, its true what's happening to me now will only magnify God's glory.

As clear as a bell these words came forth. He was back once again, and he went on.

> "And we know that all things work together for good for those that love God." Those are words of hope, Tom, it's been true my whole life as I look back on the blessings God has given me.

Right in that moment I felt the presence of Christ. It was through the text combined with my grandfather's sharing. Incredible.

Every time the word is spoken and proclaimed is a chance to know the love of God.

THE PRAYERS

As one Catholic scholar, Dr. Ralph Martin, offered, "Prayer is, at root, simply paying attention to God." This means all worship is prayer because coming before God in worship means focusing our whole being toward our Lord. Aiming everything at God:

- our voices, when we sing, sing to God;
- our hearts, when we sit in stillness, swell in love for God;
- our minds, when we contemplate the word, dwell on the divine;
- our bodies, when we stand up to be counted, stand before the Lord to be seen by him;
- our eyes, when we gaze upon the cross, fill our soul with the Lord.

And yet, we still take out time to offer explicit prayer to God to ensure we fully pay attention.

It is a time to express our mind and soul to God. But prayer also changes us. The very act of offering adoration to God changes us into beings of light. As St. Therese of Lisieux wrote,

> For me, prayer is an aspiration of the heart, it is a simple glance directed to heaven, it is a cry of gratitude and love in the midst of trial as well as joy; finally it is something great, supernatural, which expands my soul and unites me to Jesus.[3]

Like all worship, prayer has a dual power: to serve as the vessel for our praise to God, and, when done with sincerity of heart, return to us by the Spirit's blessings, awakening that divine spark within each of us.

The most extensive prayer of the day comes after the sermon. At this point in the service,

---

3. St. Therese, *The Story of a Soul*, 242.

- We are more ready to be compassionate, having understood God's compassion;
- We are ready to be bold, having seen the courage of the faithful in scripture;
- We are ready to be forgiving, having read of God's forgiveness;
- We are ready to seek justice, having seen the righteousness of God in history;
- We are ready to love all, having discovered God's love for all creation.

The Prayers of the People are meant to mobilize us to action in Christ's name.

This prayer includes words of intercession, that is, prayer concerns for our town, and the world. We ask for God's guidance for all leaders, local, national, and global.

It is meant to expand our hearts to concerns beyond our immediate reach. In 1 Timothy 2:1–5 Paul writes,

> I urge, then, first of all, that requests, prayers, intercession and thanksgiving be made for everyone—for kings and all those in authority, that we may live peaceful and quiet lives in all godliness and holiness. This is good, and pleases God our Savior.

These prayers should open our hearts to the most vulnerable and those we will never meet around the globe. It should even challenge us to call for God's grace, healing, and favor for those we might call our enemies.

Through prayer we must express our whole hearts, the doubts, fears, and all so that God can transform them by Jesus' love.

In order to underscore the power of the prayer and the hope it engenders, each prayer ends with an "amen," meaning "so be it." Everyone should join in whether audibly or silently because this act claims the prayer for your own life. It is incredibly energizing to preach in an African-American church because those "amens" level up our awareness of God's presence.

The "amen" is the equivalent of adding exclamation points in your emails. We all know people who overdo it and the email reads like it came from a crazy person or a teenage girl. But in prayer there can never be too many "amens!"

Can I get an amen?

There is, of course, far more we could say about prayer in worship. But hopefully these few observations might aid the effectiveness of your prayer time in worship.

OFFERING

The offering may have the most unrealized potential out of all our acts of worship. So much of it has become about money that we think it is simply a time to pass the plate and that the music is there to occupy our minds while we wait. But this could not be further from the truth.

Originally the time of offering was an act of atonement. "Aaron shall offer the bull as a sin-offering for himself and shall make atonement for himself and for his house" (Leviticus 16:6). Since we are on the other side of the resurrection this is no longer needed as Hebrews explains, "But as it is, [Jesus] has appeared once for all . . . to remove sin by the sacrifice of himself" (Hebrews 9:26).

No longer being a time for expiation of sins the offering is freed to be a time for us to offer, join, and grow.

> Offer yourself in thanksgiving for Christ's self-offering;
> join in God's work in the world;
> grow your faith through generosity.

Offering is not just a time to balance the budget but your way of devoting all that you are to God. It is born out of a hearing of the word, which leads to a thankful generous response, which in turn grows your faith.

Offer

In Romans Paul challenges us to give all that we are to God, "I appeal to you therefore, brothers and sisters, by the mercies of God, to present your bodies as a living sacrifice, holy and acceptable to God, which is your spiritual worship" (Romans 12:1). This means pledging our lives to God in thanksgiving.

Think about Hannah's dedication of Samuel. She was without children, deeply distressed, and prayed,

> "O Lord of hosts, if only you will look on the misery of your servant, and remember me, and not forget your servant, but will give to your servant a male child, then I will set him before you."
> (1 Samuel 1:11)

God blessed her with Samuel. In turn she dedicated him to the temple, saying, "As long as he lives, he is given to the Lord" (1 Samuel 1:28b). She dedicated her deepest treasure, Samuel, to the Lord out of thanksgiving to God. We dedicate all that we are out of joy for Christ's sacrifice of love.

Samuel literally grew up in God's house. This is not option at my church in Spartanburg. We don't have enough beds to fit everyone. Rather in order to "present our bodies as a living sacrifice to God" during the offering time we examine our heart, our minds, and our checkbooks to see if there is any part of our life that we are holding back from God.

This is one of the powers of giving your finances in worship. There are some days for me when it is easy to write the check and even add more to it. There are other days when, truthfully, it is a struggle. On those days, when I examine my heart it always discloses fear and lack of trust, some part of me that I have failed to give over to God. This means extra prayer work for the week ahead because Scripture teaches us that giving breeds blessing.

Join

The time of thanksgiving through offering is also a moment to join in the work of the Lord. Out of exultant joy for all God has done, we have the enthusiasm of the redeemed to enable others to experience the abundance of Christ's love.

Like Isaiah responding to God's question "Whom shall I send?" during the offering we exuberantly declare in our hearts, "Here I am, send me!"

Because the offering is a time to offer yourselves, we have placed the Call to Discipleship at this point in the service. After having received God's grace in confession, shared Christ's love in the Passing of the Peace, and heard God's truth in Proclamation, we are primed for service in Jesus' name.

During the offering as you are listening to the music, spend time considering specifically how you might be of service to the Lord. For instance, during the time of the coronavirus challenges that America and the world faced, your silent prayer at the offering might have gone something like this:

> *Lord, I offer my service to you.*
> *I know there are many needs in this crisis.*
> *I offer my time, my will, my strength.*
> *Show me what you would have me do,*
> *to help all those in need.*
> *Swell my heart with compassion;*
> *open my eyes to action;*
> *increase the generosity of my spirit*
> *in service to your glory.*
> *Use me as a vessel of your love*
> *to spread hope and joy.*

Grow

Finally, the offering time can be a moment of great personal growth. Proverbs 11:24 declares, "One person gives freely, yet gains even more; another withholds unduly, but comes to poverty."

Malachi 3:10 takes it even further:

> Bring the full tithe into the storehouse, so that there may be food in my house, and thus put me to the test, says the Lord of hosts; see if I will not open the windows of heaven for you and pour down for you an overflowing blessing.

In giving, God promises us an overflowing blessing!

I have heard many people share stories of financial generosity that have multiplied many times over in their lives. This is not some magical quid pro quo or a financial investment strategy, but a result of learning how not to hold anything back from God.

The return on generosity is not financial but spiritual. For when we act like our lord in self-giving love, we come to channel the Spirit's power, which inevitably fills us with joy.

I don't know if you have ever played *Guitar Hero* on Xbox, but it is a tremendous amount of fun. The idea is simple. Hit buttons on a video game controller shaped like a guitar which then automatically plays the right notes on the TV complete with adoring fans screaming their love.

My favorite song to play is "Sweet Emotion" by Aerosmith. As I hit those buttons, hear the music, and the screams of the crowd, for the briefest of moments I feel cool! Sadly, I am inevitably snapped out of my reverie by my son's mortification. "Dad, what are you doing on my Xbox!"

When we live generous lives, we channel the Spirit of Christ and come to know what it is to act like God! For God is love and when we are generous, we are being loving! And love begets love. And the more we love in this time the more others will love.

But there are two parts to this transformation—the joy and the sorrow. We not only channel God's joy in the offering but God's deep compassion and hurting heart.

Remember that it was in a time of crisis that Hannah went to the house of God in prayer in which she offered her heart's pain to God, which led her to offer her greatest blessing, which in turn led Samuel to bless the nation of Israel.

Prayer and offering go together in worship. During the offering we should be opening our heart to those suffering, alone, and in grief. We offer ourselves to God to feel their pain and to do whatever we can to relieve it.

But it is also a time for honesty, to voice our frustrations, our fears, our doubts. For even as we offer ourselves to God, "God use me as your vessel," we know there are certain things that we cannot do, that God needs to do for us. It is in times of crisis that we feel it most powerfully, like during the epidemic of the coronavirus in 2020;

> At these times the fear comes in waves.
> Will it claim my life or those I love?
> Will it decimate my finances putting me on the brink of collapse?
> Doubts trickle in:
> Would an all-powerful all loving God allow this to happen?
> Where is God?
> And frustrations mount:
> God, why are you not simply inspiring some scientist to wipe out this virus?

We may not receive an answer, but during our worship together we remind ourselves in song, in prayer, in passing the peace that in every crisis that humanity has faced God has proved faithful.

We even remember in the Apostles' Creed that Jesus went to the depths of hell for our sake, and that means that God is leaving nothing on the table in this crisis in order to carry us through.

It is in worshiping together, as the people of God, fellow followers of our Lord, that this notion takes hold so very powerfully in our hearts.

There is an amazing, even miraculous power present whenever we gather. Simply being together buoys our spirits, strengthens our resolve, and gives us the confidence of the people of God.

Think about those funerals you have been to in which amid your grief, you left with hope and confidence and a deep thankfulness for the good news of the gospel, the powerful love of Christ.

There was a precious member of my congregation, a young mother who died after a long battle with cancer. Her funeral service was incredible. Such a precious and wonderful person who loved her family so much. Before that service there was almost a crushing feeling of sorrow at how much of her life was unlived.

But during that service the prayers and the music were a healing balm. When her husband *offered* his thoughts by standing up to speak about all the angels he encountered through the care of friends, I was in awe at how powerfully the Spirit of God worked through him. And when I looked out at the congregation, I saw hundreds and hundreds of people that had come out of deep love and a desire for the good news of the gospel.

It was through his *offering* and becoming vulnerable in his grief and through the congregation *offering* its presence and worship that a palpable power of hope was created by God.

We did not leave with answers. But we left with faith, hope, and love.

CONGREGATIONAL SINGING

> Let the word of Christ dwell in you richly; teach and admonish one another in all wisdom; and with gratitude in your hearts sing psalms, hymns, and spiritual songs to God. And whatever you do, in word or deed, do everything in the name of the Lord Jesus, giving thanks to God the Father through him. (Colossians 3:16–17)

We sing in worship because Scripture shows it is a central path to express our gratitude to God. It pleases God.

Every year, I look forward to Palm Sunday. The procession of the children is truly an exultant moment in the life of the church. The sheer joy and exuberance delight my Spirit and give me a mere taste of what it might have been like for the crowd who saw Jesus' entrance into Jerusalem. Simply imagining standing on that road and waving the palms sends shivers down my spine.

This is the essence of our music in worship. It is a visceral, spontaneous eruption of joy that is born from being in the presence of our Lord, almost like an infant's squeal, an unthought eruption of delight. In fact, the "Hosanna" the crowd shouted to Jesus expresses a primal plea, "Save!"

This is how the Presbyterian *Book of Common Worship* describes it,

> With gladness, God is praised in song, for the gift of God's grace brings joy. The response may be an appropriate psalm, hymn, canticle (i.e., a biblical song other than a psalm), spiritual.[4]

This gladness is perhaps most powerfully conveyed in the throne room of heaven described in Revelation chapters 4 and 5. The scene conveys the most resplendent vision in all of Scripture. There are trumpets, rainbows, fantastic beasts, torches, lighting, thunder, thrones covered in gold, twenty-four elders casting their crowns before the throne of God, and a sea of glass. The worship begins with these four beasts singing "Holy, Holy, Holy," then angels and the elders numbering thousands upon thousands are added until finally reaching a crescendo, and John tells us,

---

4. *Book of Common Worship*, 36.

> Then I heard every creature in heaven and on earth and under the earth and in the sea, and all that is in them, singing, "To the one seated on the throne and to the Lamb be blessing and honor and glory and might for ever and ever!" And the four living creatures said, "Amen!" And the elders fell down and worshiped.
> (Revelation 5:13–14)

Our worship every week, indeed, our very lives are a dress rehearsal for this eternal praise that awaits us in heaven, just like waving those palm branches is our rehearsal for greeting Christ. That is what we are truly doing on Palm Sunday.

This makes the hymn "Holy, Holy, Holy, Lord God Almighty!" the quintessential opening song of adoration, for its words are ripped straight from Revelation—expressing the biblical act of praise with an ascendant power and joy. When the sopranos add the descant, for a moment it sounds as if we have entered the very throne room of heaven!

Amid the adoration we are fed by this sublime heavenly vision spelled out in the hymn. Perhaps you have always wondered why in this hymn the elders are "casting down their golden crowns around the glassy sea." They are casting their crowns before the throne to acknowledge that God is Lord of all. The sea is by the throne and it is glassy because it is perfectly calm. This is a sign that all the forces of evil and chaos have been defeated.

During times of crisis, such as the time in which Revelation was written, such powerful visions and praise strengthen our confidence that "this too shall be overcome!"

Every week we should begin with a hymn of praise, for adoration is the keynote of all true worship, of the creature before the Creator, of the redeemed before the Redeemer. A trend adopted about thirty years ago shifted away from this focus of praise toward a more theme-based worship. But this was a mistake, for worship, more than instructing us, is meant to be our gift to God.

This requires a dual emphasis in our singing. On the one hand, we want to offer God our very best. This means a choir that strives for excellence. They faithfully rehearse on a weekly basis to ensure quality in our gift. The music director works diligently to select appropriate anthems. The pastor and the director should work hard to ensure quality music. Quality singing shows God we care enough to make the effort.

On the other hand, as Henry Van Dyke said, "Use what talents you possess; the woods would be very silent if no birds sang there except those that sang best." The congregational singing is meant for ALL OF US to offer our voice.

The Reformed Church in America explains,

> Singing is a ministry that belongs to all the people of God. The congregation is always the primary choir. The role of professional or volunteer choirs and musicians is to aid the whole people of God in their worship.[5]

While our voice may not offer the most melodious sound, it is the heart with which we sing that our Lord measures. It gives God much delight to hear the faithful sing. We sing for the enjoyment of the Lord our God not our auditory pleasure.

There is a profound difference, as you all well know, in the energy in the sanctuary when everyone is singing!

In addition to the primary purpose of offering praise to the Lord, we sing to drive the truths of Scripture deeper into our hearts and be swayed into more faithful action. John Calvin wrote,

> There is scarcely in the world anything which is more able to turn or bend this way and that the morals of men, as Plato prudently considered it. And in fact, we find by experience that it has a sacred and almost incredible power to move hearts in one way or another.[6]

The hymn "My Shepherd Will Supply My Need" makes me feel the shepherding love of God whenever I sing it. "What Child Is This," with its gentle tune puts me at the foot of the manger. But perhaps no other hymn so powerfully opens Scripture to me as "Were You There When They Crucified My Lord." It makes me feel

> like I was there
> > to hear the nails pounded into his flesh;
> like I was there
> > to see them pierce him in his side;
> like I was there
> > when the sun refused to shine;
> like I was there
> > when they laid him in the tomb.

The gasp of agony when you sing "O ... O ... O!" indeed makes me tremble with terror, dread, and shock.

---

5. "Theology and Place of Music," para. 8.
6. Calvin, *Preface*, para. 9.

The power of singing strengthens our faith and gives us courage in times of fear, hope in despair, clarity of conviction in times of confusion, and divine joy in times of celebration.

If singing has the power to support the faithful it also has the power to convert the doubtful. Paul sang in prison, which served as a testament to the others in prison with him. The text tells us they were listening, and you never know should someone hear you sing how it might open God's truth to them. Martin Luther said, "He must cheerfully sing and talk about this, that others might hear it and come to Christ."[7]

Finally, singing the faith has a supernatural power, that is a power by the Holy Spirit, to connect us not only to God but to one another. The YouTube videos of Italians singing from their balconies during the coronavirus were incredibly heartening. Song ties people together across distances, across race, economics, and even faith.

For those of you who have been to a community thanksgiving service you know what I am talking about. At the one in Spartanburg there are many people I know but usually hundreds of people I do not. Most every year the closing hymn is "Let There Be Peace on Earth." It speaks to the call for each of us to be agents of peace through the knowledge that we are all God's children.

To hear all our voices, even those of different faiths, all praising God together creates this profound moment of kinship, kindles my love for them, and opens me to have a keener respect for their perspectives on faith and life.

THE LORD'S SUPPER

The table we approach on Communion Sundays is the table from which Jesus unfolded the deepest truths to his closest friends in John's Gospel; on that night he told them this is the table . . .

> in which we discover he no longer calls us servants but friends;
> in which we learn the greatest love is one in which you give your life for another;
> in which we learn Jesus promises a mansion
> that is a home in heaven with God!

If you can understand what happens at the table, then you are most of the way to discovering the full power of the hour. The text we turn to is that simple yet profoundly complex and rich invitation from our Lord in Luke's

---

7. Luther, "Preface," 333.

Gospel, during that last meal he had with his disciples in the upper room when he instituted the Lord's Supper,

"This, do in remembrance of me" (Luke 22:19).

> This, all of this,
> the words,
> the bread,
> the cup,
> do it when you remember me.

The word Jesus used for memory, *anamnesis*, has a depth of meaning not fully captured by our English word, especially when it comes to this sacred meal. It refers to the memorial meal Jesus instituted but in such a way that we participate in its mystery, in which past, present, and future are all NOW at this table.

> It is a table of past sacrifice,
> present comfort,
> and future joy
> all intermingled into a single moment by the powerful Spirit of God.

Anamnesis Part 1: The Past Sacrifice of Love

God has always provided sacred remembering such as when the bow was put in the cloud after the flood. Every time we see the rainbow, we are to remember the divine promise to never again destroy the earth by flood. At the last plague upon Egypt God declared of the Passover, "This day shall be a day of remembrance for you." When Jesus commands us to do *this*, he means to take us back to the moment with his disciples so long ago.

It is to be a sacred and solemn remembering of his sacrifice of love. As he tells us in Matthew 26:28, "[This is] my blood of the covenant, which is poured out for many for forgiveness of sins." Paul commands us to examine ourselves and only then eat the bread and drink the cup. I am to remember, you are to remember, that Christ went up on the cross because of my sins.

For many people Maundy Thursday, that service during Holy Week that reenacts the very night Jesus instituted this meal, is their favorite service of the year. Not because it is joyful but because of its power of solemn memory to take us back to that holy night. Communion on this night has a deep, resonant power enabling us to grieve our sins, feel the weight of them placed on the shoulders of our Lord, and to see the depth of his love.

Every year, before this service, I listen to Handel's "Surely, He Hath Born Our Griefs." The biblical text combined with the haunting music prepare my heart and mind for what I know will happen on that night.

When we come to this table, we should come with the past sacrifice of Christ in mind. But there is more. Much more.

Anamnesis Part 2: The Present Comfort of His Real Presence

According to one pastor, "Remembrance activates the past for the present."[8] This is the same type of remembering the Jews do in Passover. Even today, thousands of years later, a Jewish father recites Exodus 13:8, "You shall tell your child on that day, 'It is because of what the Lord did for me when I came out of Egypt.'" Even though they were not alive at the time of the exodus, nevertheless, there is a powerful sense that God's Passover delivered them.

As Presbyterians when the bread is broken, the wine is poured, and we recite Jesus' words, "This is my body; this is my blood," we believe that Christ truly is present in that bread and wine. It is not transformed, it is still bread and wine, but by the mysterious power of the Holy Spirit, the real presence of Christ is found.

It is what happened to two disciples walking on the road to Emmaus, with the resurrected Jesus. They did not know it was him, but Luke tells us that when Jesus broke the bread, "Then their eyes were opened and they recognized him" (Luke 24:31).

In this meal we are eating it with the Lord, right now, not just remembering the past. And despite our sins, we need not come in fear. In this meal Jesus tells us, "I no longer call you servants but friends." We approach a table of fellowship with friends, not an altar of sacrifice. Jesus calls to us from Matthew, "Come to me all you who are carrying heavy burdens." The real presence of Christ offers us tremendous comfort right now.

In this meal, Presbyterians, perhaps more than any other aspect, emphasize the present welcome of Christ which unifies us to friends, families, and all the faithful.

This makes the feast a deep moment of exceeding joy as all hope is realized. In it we discover *Nachat Ruach*, a marvelous phrase my rabbi friend in Birmingham taught me, which means spiritual delight. It is when a moment in time is frozen in sheer rapturous harmony through the powerful presence of God. He used it describe one afternoon with his wife and two children in which they just spent time laughing and talking and eating

---

8. Sutton, "The Bible and Anamnesis," para. 10.

and remembering younger days. It was the perfect afternoon, and as time stopped, he was filled with an overwhelming love and joy.

When we celebrate World Communion Sunday, we know that same spiritual delight. And as the hundreds of people stream forward for intinction, I can almost see, the people from Brazil, Russia, Thailand, England, and more all making their way to the same table with our Lord at the center. It is a moment of incredible power and unity.

As we come to this table thankful for the past and comforted by our Lord's presence, now in spiritual joy our faith in the future becomes as solid as the Rock of our Lord Jesus Christ.

Anamnesis Part 3: Hope for the Future.

When we celebrate this meal, we remember that at the last supper, Jesus promised his disciples, "I tell you, I will never again drink of this fruit of the vine until that day when I drink it new with you in my Father's kingdom" (Matthew 26:29). Not only did he promise to be at this table again in heaven but on that same night with his disciples he promised them a place in heaven and that he himself would come to take them there.

As John Calvin taught, more than Christ being brought down, we are lifted heavenward in this supper celebrating the eternal feast with our Lord. It is THE heavenly banquet in which this table becomes wide enough and grand enough to hold all the faithful from every time and place!

And when we receive this meal, as if from our Lord's hand, that is when we remember the future and past, present and future all dissolve into NOW, no matter what grief or loss may hang in our heart.

Albert Einstein had a deep love for his dearest friend, Michele Besso. The bond began when they were students, which then grew during their work together in the Bern patent office. They would walk home together discussing scientific subjects as thoughts of everyday life would melt away. He kept up correspondence with him throughout his life, but the last letter was written when his best friend in life died. It was a letter of condolence to the family, which disclosed his deep spirituality and a yearning for the mysterious.

> Now Besso has departed from this strange world a little ahead of me. That means nothing. People like us, who believe in physics, know that the distinction between past, present, and future is only a stubbornly persistent illusion.[9]

9. Albert Einstein, quoted in "Einstein Believed," para. 4.

I have seen that illusion dissolve away in the faces of those who come to the table.

> Perhaps your beloved spouse
> of sixty years recently left this world;
> maybe it is your dear mother you remember,
> that you laid to rest one year ago to the day;
> it could be a dear friend who offered you so much support
> for so long,
> who stood by you
> every step of the way;
> and as you step toward the bread
> and dip it in the cup,
> on a rare occasion, I have seen those tears of sorrow
> turn into joy,
> as you know, right now, by the power of our Lord,
> your husband, your mother, your friend
> is drinking from that very same cup.

Remember the loving sacrifice of our Lord, the comfort of his real presence right now, and the realized future hope whenever you come to this meal.

8

Key Themes for Congregations

Now that we have explored the paths for individuals to cultivate the experience of God, next we will examine key barriers and critical factors for congregations to more effectively grow their role in connecting people to the divine.

As I conducted one focus group after the next, there were several threads that carried through each of them.

- The blessing and power of children in worship
- The ways we might reach those that are spiritual but not religious
- The hunger for authenticity and vulnerability

DON'T FORGET THE CHILDREN . . . AND YOUTH

Perhaps the greatest surprise for me were the dozens of unprompted examples people shared about experiencing God through children. The stories came as answers to the open-ended question, "Where do you experience God in church?" The examples came from parents, grandparents, youth, singles, married, divorced, those with several children, and those who never had children of their own.

After the second focus group, it quickly became clear that children are not only critical for the future of the church, but they are a key entry point into people's experience of God. There were many phrases that exemplified this sentiment:

- "I feel closer during the children's message than any other time because I see it in their faces."
- "[The children's time] hits me right. It is simple; that helps me. It is aimed at children, who are the future of the church."
- "For me the children, what they do and say is authentic. It is unfiltered; they don't know to think, "How should I say this?" Sometimes it is humorous, but it is the content and the way they say it."
- "There is a joyfulness there . . . in the children; that's how you merge joyful and celebratory."
- "The girls would say, "Did you hear what the pastor said?!" . . . As parents, that was the best!"

As I listened to these quotes and stories, it was clear there were different expectations for the children vs. the adults. For adult-led music, exceptional quality was important.

But if it was youth, people were moved regardless of the quality. One person explained,

> Because they have the courage to try . . . little kids played "Jingle Bells" in church and it was okay. The fact that children want to help lead, even if they mess it up. It is training disciples, teaching them a willingness to come forward.

I was surprised when she told me that "Jingle Bells" was played at the Christmas Eve service. I thought, "Should the children play a secular song on such an important day?" And then she offered the perfect explanation that convinced me, "They are in fifth grade, and that song brought their gift to the Christ child. It was their gift."

It seems several factors are playing into people's experience of God through the children. They admired their courage. The willingness to play the piano, read a Scripture, or perform a play in front of hundreds of people and to do it for God gives them great hope. As one person explained about seeing children come forward during children's time, "I find a joy in the ones who are hesitant, because of their vulnerability. They are asking themselves, 'Do I belong? Will I fit in? Am I safe?'" It was clear this person had her own hesitancies and fears about whether she belonged, but seeing the children's courage gave her courage.

Children's time was also a moment to be reminded of God's special care through the parents. One person said, "Just seeing the parent go down with the child and sit close to make sure child is okay . . . it's pretty neat."

That simple, watchful love reminded them of God's providence that gives us both freedom and protection.

Another person recognized that the whole congregation watches the children carefully, "The child chimes the hour, and everyone is counting along with them." Through the children, people process their own fears and hopes before God.

The enthusiasm and the joy the children bring opens their hearts. "To see the kids up there, often enthralled, shows me that God is there. I have never had a bright-light experience of God showing himself to me but seeing the light in the kids' face lets me know God is [real]."

Their innocence and what that leads to endears people, "When youth sing that always gets you; for me the innocence so often with youth. They don't have as many experiences as us; their faith is not muddled or questioned."

This sense of innocence leads to an experience of the profoundness in the simple things of faith, "One thing I notice at the end of children's time. We do a repeat-after-me prayer. As the kids say it, they remind us of the basics of our faith and, at the end of the day, that is all we need."

But hearing the young people share their faith offered moments of great hope. As with this person's example, "For those of us who do not go overseas on mission trips, the people who went share it back with the congregation. I loved it from the young people. It is a great way to experience God, knowing the children are connected to God."

However, even as people spoke of the children's innocence and lack of worldly experience, they offered counter examples.

The first was more light-hearted. In one congregation each month the children and youth write the liturgy at the end of a weekend fun night. One focus group broke into laughter recalling one particular confession as a man said, "The prayers they write are very honest. . . . 'Forgive us for the things we have done and the things we thought about doing.'"

The second example was more heartbreaking. One teacher spoke of the hardship her students face, "Some youth may not have had the opportunity to go to church . . . the ones with abortions in the fifth grade."

Her example was about the power of connecting to children and youth within poverty, abuse, and violence. She found it especially meaningful to be involved in connecting them to God because she knew the power of the divine to break through the past and bring hope. She had seen their resilience and the hope in the smallest acts of kindness.

In those surprising God moments with children, either light- or heavy-hearted, we discover the children's willingness to be honest about things we struggle with but don't realize it because we spend too much effort suppressing the very thought. These moments of divine surprise through the children are often about fundamental aspects of the human condition that we have anesthetized ourselves to through the years.

This is the place in which the children's impact and the need for authenticity and vulnerability overlap. People find so much power in the children because it is in the children that they see more willingness than they do in themselves or other adults, a willingness to be vulnerable before God, and that courage gives them hope.

For example, we want to live in a world of greater acceptance and equality. We want to be in a world in which we can connect to people regardless of background. One mother brought her son to a soup kitchen for homeless families. She thought about taking the time to explain beforehand about how his life was different from theirs.

> I was going to tell him the "dos" and "don'ts," but I never got around to it. Thank goodness! The homeless children and my son just played with each other; it was straight on. . . . All these worries just went away when the kids just played with each other.

REACHING THE "SPIRITUAL BUT NOT RELIGIOUS"

More and more people seem to be drifting away from church or never grew up in church at all. There has been a tremendous amount written about this, and I wanted to learn something more about the people who believe in God in some form or fashion and what, if anything, the church might do to connect them to God.

Some key conversations on a cross country train trip along with casual conversations in Chicago offered key insights.

One evening I had a very compelling conversation at dinner on the train with a Native-American rights lawyer who had successfully argued before the Supreme Court.

I saw some similarities with this woman and a child psychiatrist I met in Chicago. Both are very successful in their fields, but neither are churchgoers. They shared passionately though about their sense of calling in the world and their love of nature. For one reason or another, neither had a traditional faith or a traditional doctrinal belief.

Even so, they both had a spirituality that was important to them. The lawyer commented that she belonged to the church of "the great outdoors." She and her husband summer in Colorado every year. She said upon her death she would love to have her ashes sprinkled in her basil garden by her house.

The question that is growing in my heart is this: is there a way that the church can help this population experience God? Of course, we know there are millions and millions like this in our country and thousands in our own communities.

How can the church support these people in their quest for meaning, hope, and service in a way that respects their faith journey without compromising our beliefs? Though I think it is a difficult question, I truly believe there is a way.

I spent time chatting with a very friendly couple from Tucson, Arizona, who moved to Chico, California. They moved to get out of the heat and find a simpler life. The wife didn't like keeping house, so she made sure their newly built home was only seven hundred square feet. The husband said his work shed was three times the size of the house!

He was a truck driver that drove triples. That's three trailers that he drove on icy roads through Idaho, Utah, and Nevada for thirty years. He rides a Harley and attends Calvary churches. He told me, "I have a patch on my biker vest that says, 'These are my church clothes.'"

It seems coming to church in a way that is comfortable is essential for him. I asked him what he thought congregations could do to be more relevant and helpful, and he told me, "I had a friend who came to visit who never found a group. Too many cliques in the church. . . . Make everyone feel welcome!" His comments echoed the need for authenticity I had already heard from very churched people. The desire to be themselves before God in their place of sacredness is essential.

His wife was not a person of traditional faith. She said,

> He goes to church, but it is not for me. Someone telling me what to do means nothing to me. Some big guy up there telling me what to do is not for me, but seeing a bird or being in my garden that means something. . . . It is like a gift. It depends on what you see. I just need to be in my garden.

This is the same theme from the high-powered people I met before! There are times the church needs to teach "right doctrine." But that is not our only calling, nor was it Jesus' only path to reach people with God's love.

It seems urgent that the church find more effective ways to speak to the spirituality that lies within each person.

Many of these people have left the church or never came to it to begin with. It is because of both the severe judgmentalism they perceive and the inauthentic environment in the church itself. Sometimes this is misperception and sometimes it is tragically too accurate.

We are made to be in a relationship with God and to be connected to the divine. All humans yearn for this, even those who consider themselves not religious; they ache for a more spiritual experience in life, often finding it through nature, and describe it as a peace and a wholeness.

One person expressed this thought:

> I would want a program to connect people more deeply. I would want to set up something founded on creativity and spontaneity. . . . There is a group in Western North Carolina called "A Sanctified Art." . . . They also resource intergenerational art projects. They put out bundles; they have artists, poets, and technology. They create unique, experiential things for congregations. It has been profound.

Art and nature could be the place that welcomes non-church people into our congregations. One church has a serenity garden. One woman's experience there resonated with the yearning expressed by the non-churchgoers I encountered.

> Sometimes the quietest places I have been is where I can experience God in a greater way. Like the serenity garden, it is a perfect place. I can take the time to be still. When issues have come up in my life it is a place of tranquility. A lot of people have put in a lot of time to make the garden special. It is more than just pretty; everything out there is meaningful, honoring someone alive or dead. It makes the church something more.

This serenity garden has elements connected to members of the congregation. But a church could build a community serenity garden that could have elements to welcome all types of people.

Clearly the love of nature is the place of commonality between people of traditional faith and those with more personal beliefs. Perhaps that is a place to start.

But the boldest, most playful, and creative example to reach the unchurched comes unsurprisingly from San Francisco, although the man himself is from Georgia.

This was a pastor who had conducted a steampunk wedding. If you don't know what steampunk is, google it. You are in for a surprise! It is a combination of anachronistic steam-powered technology with leather, metal, science fiction, and Victorian fashion!

Early in this pastor's ministerial career, he had baptized an infant boy, and over the years, he kept in touch with the family and the young man. This young man had drifted from the church, but they always stayed in touch. The man wanted this pastor to perform his wedding. His wife was not a person of traditional faith, but he could marry them because, as he said, they saw him as a person and a friend not so much as a pastor.

> It was not in a church. I was dressed in steampunk. I wanted to honor their wishes and my faith. I dressed up as Doc Brown from the third *Back to Future* movie.

The pastor did the voice from the priest in the *Princess Bride* in the opening of the ceremony and Doc Brown's voice during the vows. He inserted God language and faith at key moments and talked about God when he explained why we have weddings. And there was both Scripture and Bruce Springsteen.

Clearly, this pastor has a gift for creativity and reaching those not of traditional ways of connecting to God. But it was all possible only because of the trust and the relationship that was already there.

If we want to reach the unchurched, we need to begin with mutual respect and connecting based on friendship.

A MAJOR BARRIER: THE IMPORTANCE AND CHALLENGE OF VULNERABILITY AND AUTHENTICITY

This recurring theme throughout the focus groups was surprising and compelling. If there is one thing our Presbyterian churches are sorely lacking in, is the freedom for people to be fully themselves without fear of being judged or excluded. In fact, in the survey you may have noted this was ranked quite low (55!).

Because of the success orientation of our culture, people from every walk of life found it impossible to share their whole selves. At the same time, this sharing proved critical for growing deep community amongst the churches. If there was one thing we could change in our churches that would both grow our members' attendance and draw in others from the community, this is it. Figuring out how to do this should be a top priority because it is through being vulnerable that we experience God.

Failing to fully share ourselves with others often means we have not been honest with ourselves—or God—about our struggles, our demons, and broken places. It is in opening ourselves up to others that we finally learn who we are. This open reflection removes the barriers and defenses we have erected, which allows God in.

I find myself wanting to be in both worlds, in the life of the mind and the experiential life. I want to go there, but I have a hard time being vulnerable. So, I find it needs to come in smaller places in my life, with a few trusted church members, my clergy colleagues, my family, and most of all, my wife, Wendy.

But in the church, this failure of being vulnerable creates a level of mistrust. It leads people to think folks are not being authentic and that they are putting on a false front. I have had one church member and friend tell me when I was wearing jeans and a golf shirt to church supper say, "I like this look. It makes you look human!" We tell ourselves every week that we are a community of broken sinners, every one of us in need of God's grace, and yet, virtually everyone wears a mask of some sort in their church life.

This is how one woman explained the challenge . . .

> I don't think this church encourages vulnerability. . . . It is very difficult; it will be [seen] as weakness. . . . I do appreciate it from the pulpit, but I don't see it from the pew. . . . As Presbyterians we think being vulnerable is one step away from handling snakes. Sometimes people come right up to the door of sharing and then they step back.

Often the key to growing a vulnerable congregation is for the pastor to be vulnerable, though clearly, from the quote above, not everyone believes it will make a great difference. But one pastor found it to be the case in their ministry.

This pastor has experienced hardship and personal demons but doesn't hide them.

> Sometimes in church we think we have to put on the happy face, but we don't. . . . [We can] show brokenness in church. . . . Buechner says church could learn from AA. I share a lot of personal brokenness and I get more comments, "Could I come to your office and talk to you?" It is about hard things. When we are willing to be authentic it might lead to that. . . . In my own brokenness, I experience God.

Another church member said, "If the pastor is relatable it makes a difference. My pastor told the story of a personal hardship." The pastor was new at the time and invited this congregant and others to find a place of connection. A few other pastors said things like, "I think it can be modeled in the pulpit," "I shared about a panic attack, and more people felt connected to me." Another told about the passing of their father, and still another said, "I was a weepy puddle on Sunday during the sermon, but it made a lot of connections."

No matter the topic, the outcome was the same. Whenever the pastor shared deeply from the well of their trials, the congregants felt a deeper connection and then experienced God more consistently not only on that day, but for years to come.

Of course, being vulnerable requires risk and sometimes the pastor suffers repercussions from divergent experiences from the same event. One group told me about such a time in Sunday worship. The pastor opened the floor to people in the pews to share thoughts about their community (this idea terrified me!).

People offered their honest, heartfelt reflections. The pastor has done an excellent job being vulnerable herself, and so folks felt free to do so themselves. Overall, it was very moving, but not without conflict. Even though it is a multi-ethnic church, the friction did not occur along racial lines, but generational ones. One participant declared, "There were also people that were livid; who wanted to put the lid on that. . . . Don't suggest that we are not good. . . ." This older, African-American church member felt like this type of sharing became an opportunity for the younger progressives to judge the traditional older members.

There are ways to break down these walls, and the focus groups divulged several. Small groups seem to be a key place, as one woman said, "I think it has a better probability in very small groups on specific topics in those discussions that build trust. I have a net. . . . Here, people won't think you are nuts."

One person described a Bible study in which she had such an experience.

> Being born again . . . a lot of people got beat over the head because we were told we are not Christian. . . . But when we start talking about being born again as seeing a new way of living in God . . . and that belief is more about trust, God becomes more powerful . . . people yearn for church language to be unpacked.

It was through the unpacking of the text that opened them to God in a way that allowed them to be fully themselves before God and each other. She concluded by saying,

> They are eating it up; a lot of people are hungry for authentic Christianity—more authentic, more real.

Someone found their yearning for authenticity in Sunday school,

> I think this is a safe place. We were drawn here when we were visiting other churches. We walked into Sunday school and the people were so real; they were arguing, 'fun' arguing, back and forth about something. It was not stuffy; topics were not off limits.... Everybody has the freedom to be who they are and do not have to agree to express questions, concerns, and doubts.

Another church had obviously done an excellent job cultivating a spirit of mutual acceptance. This is how they described their experience, "A lot of that comes from the knowledge that you are here with the same foundation, even if you disagree, the end goal is to be Christlike people. It is safe because the end goal is the same." This person joined the church determined not to put on a false front. She was going to be herself no matter what, and it worked. "I thought, 'I am going to be who I am . . . I will be accepted, or I won't.' It was so refreshing. . . . And we found the differences do not matter so much; there is love and compassion even if you are new."

Several people shared their experience of recovering from addictions or of that experience from friends. One person experienced God powerfully outside the church with others also recovering. They said,

> When someone says they have no God in their life, and I can see they clearly have [I see it] in how they share with me. . . . It is amazing how things work in their life. . . . It can only be through God's power. . . . I tell them that is God that did that; then I share after with them . . . powerful forgiveness and reconciliation.

Another church professional found the greatest level of vulnerability outside of the church, and it had a profound impact.

> It is so much about vulnerability. It is so important. I have had a relationship that has brought me to a lot of unchurched people who are vulnerable that I do not find around the church a lot . . . and it has opened me to an experience of God greater than I have ever had.

This person proceeded to explain it was a community of people who had left the church. There was a deep willingness to discuss and share faith, and he said, "My faith has deepened so much . . . to accept a much bigger God without boundaries."

It was clear this group was life-changing for him, but the great tragedy was spoken in his next words.

> The huge majority consider themselves Christians but are unchurched because they see themselves as judged by the church . . . because they have addictions or crime issues. It is hard for

> people to come into an environment in which people seem they have it together.

How deeply sad that, in order to find their faith and express it openly, they had to leave the church.

Part of being able to be authentic is being in a community that accepts diverse types of people. But sometimes this means exchanging one set of judgments for another. One African-American woman expressed this frustration. She felt her church had become too political and left the Bible behind.

> It is important to read the Bible; it really tells you how to live. . . . On a daily basis you slip up; churches have become too political. . . . They kept a balance before in the black church.

This view in her church put her at odds with the younger generation.

> We are diverse, but not inclusive. . . . We all experience things in different ways, there are a lot of "isms" and that depends on how you are treated. . . . So, some will pass the peace with me in church but not talk to me on the street. How does the church encourage people to live like the Bible tells us to live?

It is always a challenge for a church to be prophetic and welcoming at the same time. Turning to Christ's example in the Scriptures is the best model for us.

Some churches see the call for more justice in the world, and certainly we absolutely need that. Yes! But following Christ's path for a more just world is the one we are called to. For an authentic church, we need to explore the possibility that there is a distinction between being "political" and working to create a more just world. What do we see in Jesus' life that would help us discover this path?

People don't want church to simply reflect the world. So, is there a way to thread the needle?

Authenticity, welcome, and love in all things is the hope for the church. And, in the end, the leaders set the tone. As one pastor said, "I have a lot of hope for the spoken word. . . . We should be willing to ask the question . . . 'Are you broken?'"

9

Conclusions

THESE FOCUS GROUPS AND interviews and the survey have convinced me that God is powerfully present in the lives of many. I am also convinced that there is a tremendous amount we can do to help people connect more deeply and powerfully to the divine.

At one level, we must begin with the faith and trust that God is powerfully active in the world and in people's lives. As congregations, pastors, and leaders, we can create an expectancy in all aspects of the church life that God is going to powerfully present. This expectancy must grow from an authentic, personal connection with God that flows forth from the leaders of the church. But this also requires a humble vulnerability. Otherwise, church members might perceive that the experience of God is only for those with perfect lives and strong faiths. It is often through the vulnerability of pastors that people feel safe to believe in their hearts that God will be with them as well.

Teaching them to expect God to show up also means teaching them how to recognize God. Several members described how powerfully a seven-year Bible study helped them in this way. As one woman said,

> It made you get to know God. You saw how he worked through the ages. It opened my eyes to how he was working in my life. Take Abraham, God told him to just leave and he went. When a chance arose to lead the children's Wednesday program, I knew God was wanting me to step out and faith and do it.

Along with setting a stage of expectation and teaching people to recognize God, we need to focus on preaching a God that is big enough. People will quickly see through the façade of a God that is simply a reflection of the latest political fad, whether it is from a conservative or progressive point of view. People are not coming to church to have what they hear on the news rehashed in worship. They want the godly point of view which can only spring from the pages of Scripture. Though the church needs to address the deep issues that confront society, it should be addressing them in a different way, a way that reflects the life of our Lord.

Next, most Protestant churches, and certainly Presbyterian ones, miss the opportunity to use the liturgy more intentionally to connect people to God. In the beginning of this paper we saw that people experience God in at least seven different ways: Holy Presence, Holy Communion, Holy Revelation, Holy Purpose, Holy Power and Providence, Holy Grace, and Holy Love.

As I think about Presbyterian worship, it may be we put too much emphasis on truth, that is Holy Revelation, and not enough on the others. All the different ways people experience God are present in our worship services, but they are underplayed.

Don't underestimate the opening of worship.

It is a place to set powerful expectations of the presence of God through words, silence, and music. Weaving those three elements to move people out of the frenetic pace of their lives into a place in which they expect to encounter God is critical to the experience of God in worship.

Spend more time constructing the confession sequence.

This is clearly a lost opportunity. If people are looking for a place of greater vulnerability and authenticity, then this is the place in which theoretically we come before God with our broken selves. The problem is that I think this section rarely has the intended effect. One person found a problem with wording of the confessions. She thought more biblical-based and poetic confessions would help. The introduction to the confession is the place we can spend more time leading people into the mindset and the "heartset" of confession. The same works with the assurance of pardon, followed by the musical response. Make sure each section is maximized.

Silence is underutilized in our worship services. Spend more time constructing moments of silence throughout the worship services that give people time to reflect and absorb the music, the words, and the sacraments.

Make congregational singing more "singable."

Congregational singing was critical for almost every participant in the focus groups. But virtually every congregation I have attended has a great deal of trouble fully engaging the congregation in the hymns, especially for those who sit in the back! At some point in our worship planning, Presbyterian churches started putting a great emphasis on a cohesive theme throughout worship. And, indeed, people find this very meaningful. However, we have erred entirely too heavily on these themes to the detriment of the hymns. If people aren't singing them, they aren't connecting to the theme of the day.

More importantly, the purpose of congregational singing is not connecting to a theme. It is to draw that non-rational part of ourselves to experience God through the music in a way the words cannot. A return to the primary purpose of congregational singing could go a long way to helping people experience God through worship.

Next, learning to sing as a congregation takes work. Many people did not grow up Presbyterian or in church at all. Also teaching people to sing is less prominent in our society than it once was. Congregations should spend more time simply teaching people how to sing and particularly how to sing the great hymns of the church.

Be sure to give people "the dinner."

About worship one person said, "Many funerals are 'He was a nice guy and he's dead and we are sad, but he is in heaven, but it is all okay.' . . . That is a popsicle. Where is the dinner?"

He explained his comment,

> Several years ago, when my young niece died in her sleep, I was to speak, and I picked up the microphone and turned around at the packed congregation and the weight of that was huge . . . but I also had a feeling they were saying, "Tell us something that we can latch onto, something that is going to make this a little bit better." They were ready . . . they were really hoping. People come to church with one question . . . "Is it true?" and the sermon was, "Yes, it is true!" . . . their belief, their hope made you feel the presence of God; it was in the hope.

Virtually everyone is yearning to experience more God in their lives. The call of the church and the call of every one of Christ's followers is to this wondrous God. Make sure by the time the worship concludes people are not asking . . . "Where was God?"

If people find themselves asking that question, we know, as leaders of the church, we have fundamentally led people astray. For there is another barrier, unseen, that blocks vulnerability and allows us to control a puppet God of our own making rather than be impacted by the Lord of all.

Worship a Living God rather than a Golden Calf.

> Jesus answered them, "You are wrong, because you know neither the scriptures nor the power of God. For in the resurrection they neither marry nor are given in marriage, but are like angels in heaven. And as for the resurrection of the dead, have you not read what was said to you by God, 'I am the God of Abraham, the God of Isaac, and the God of Jacob'? He is God not of the dead, but of the living." And when the crowd heard it, they were astounded at his teaching. (Matthew 22:29–33)

Jesus had some interesting encounters with the religious authorities of the day. After this debate on resurrection he so thoroughly defeats them that we are told, "They no longer dared ask him any questions." Clearly, when we oppose the Lord not all encounters with God are pleasant. And since the topic of the debate, the resurrection of the dead, is so thoroughly settled in the Christian faith, the passage at first glance might not seem to have anything to teach us. There is at least one intriguing point here about the next life. "In heaven, they neither marry nor are given in marriage." In one Bible study, a young couple told me that this was unimaginable and sad, but later the wife of a more seasoned couple said, "Thank goodness one lifetime is enough!"

But there is another subtle phrase that has far more implications for experiencing God than we might at first think: "Now he is God not of the dead, but of the living"! "A God of the living" has consequences for our understanding of God, the nature of Scripture, and our own practice of faith.

First, in order to be a God of the living, God's self must be alive as well! A living God does not reside in the pages of a book under our interpretive control but in the world and in our lives.

Every few weeks I practically die of a heart attack in my house. Usually, it's in the nighttime when I sneak to the kitchen for a midnight snack. I grab something from the fridge when a shadow catches the corner of my eye. I pause for a moment when suddenly, a blurry, furry ball of midnight black lightning leaps across my path. It is our cat, Kidden, K-I-D-D-E-N (blame our daughter, Liz, for the name . . .) whose beautiful fur allows her to blend into the night. Now, I know she is always actively prowling at night, but she still makes me jump a mile.

We love dogs because they fit into our lives so very well. But cats are different. You must fit into their lives. Cats are such delightfully irksome pets because they cannot be tamed, and even when Kidden nestles up to me for a pet, occasionally she still gives me a swipe of her claws to remind me of my place.

A living God cannot be tamed by our theology or doctrine. A living God is out there poking, prodding, and actively prowling about and at any moment the Lord can leap into your life, sucking their air from your lungs with amazing delight or demanding your life . . . and just as with your cats you never know when it might happen!

One person had this experience with a broken watch. She was sorting through her husband's things after a long, debilitating illness had taken him from her. She came across his old watch. This old watch happened to be stuck on the exact time he had died. She gasped for breath as she remembered. For some this might have been an impossibly hard reminder. But the Holy Spirit came upon her with such peace that it became a gift to her that right in that moment of loss, that exact time, God was with her.

Of course, a living God also means a living word. Not only does God not reside in a book but neither does God's word reside in the pages of the book. This one is tricky but very important. I know it is confusing because we call the Bible the word of God. But in fact, that book only comes to life as God's word to us when it is read dynamically, through the power of the Holy Spirit.

When we act like those words on the page are carved into eternal, ageless stone, we ossify God's Spirit in our hearts which leads to

- condoning slavery,
- condemning all non-Christians to hell,
- and paving the way to all the worst behaviors humans can imagine.

This has profound implications for the role of Scripture in the practice of faith. Tradition is a critical component of any life of faith. It is necessary in order to cultivate deep patterns of belief. Just like playing the scales on a piano embeds those keys into your hands and soul, so do the traditions of our faith.

As a result, within the pages of Scripture God *commands* a tremendous number of practices into Israel, the chosen people of God. The Old Testament literally has hundreds of them and perhaps unique in all the world, the Jewish people, though few, have survived through some of the greatest horrors in history precisely through the strength of their traditions.

But despite this deep reverence for tradition, their reading of Scripture is also fully alive.

By its very essence life responds and adapts to its environment lest it die; life must grow, and when it stops growing it starts dying.

The faith is ever growing, but like a majestic tree it put down roots long ago that are strong and networked, and everything that grows today depends upon a stout trunk to hold it up; so the branches grow wider and wider.

For the Jews their strong trunk is made of the Lordship of the one almighty and everlasting God, the Passover, the Ten Commandments and the Shema. This core allows even strong branches to fall away, like the temple, without losing the whole tree.

For scores of generations their faith included ritual animal sacrifice and elaborate temple worship. But today, those are actions long past.

Such a thing would have been unimaginable to them two thousand years ago. But when the temple was destroyed in AD 70 their faith dramatically changed and adapted but they didn't lose the core.

The Christian faith grows from the central trunk of the Lordship of Jesus Christ and his life, death, and resurrection. Jesus told us that at the very base of the tree of faith are the two laws: love God and love your neighbor as yourself.

From this amazing foundation literally hundreds of branches from the Catholics, to the Orthodox, to the Protestants, and more have grown into a glorious behemoth with many gnarled and twisty branches. Thus, even though the Bible does not change (we do not revise it as we go along), the way in which each age of faith obeys it does. But not according to its own whims but in reliance on the Holy Spirit.

This means when I read Scripture today, I am not only trying to learn for example what Paul was telling the Romans, but what God is teaching me, right now! This leads to our third implication for our key phrase.

My faith, and your faith, alive!

> The power of a God fully alive
> discovered through a word fully alive,
> leads to a life as fully
> and wondrously alive
> as that moment
> when God created everything
> and declared it was VERY GOOD.

The notion of a living God tells us something not just about God but about our life. We live a life that borrows from the kind of "life" God has.

It is fundamental and at the root of what it means to be alive. Think of the expression to be "fully alive." It means our senses our keener. We experience our breath, our sight, and hearing and heartbeat with greater intensity and awareness.

So, to think of God as the Living God is to first realize our own life is but a shadow of the kind of supercharged life God has in mind for us. We are living lives in shades of gray when God urges us to know the depth and breadth of color life has to offer.

> But before we can embrace this life fully alive,
> we must be ready to admit the many gods we have erected.
> Like the shiny, beautiful golden calf
> they are alluring
> and captivating,
> and distracting,
> but also just as lifeless, dead, and powerless.
>
> For many years I worshiped the god
> of theological correctness,
> intellectual prowess,
> personal competence,
> and self-righteous judgment.
> I remember arguing so forcefully in youth group
> that I made someone cry,
> > but I didn't care
> > because I was right,
> > and I was . . .
> I was right.
>
> I still don't know why I thought it was so important
> to prove my point,
> to try to prove that I was smarter
> and better.
>
> But the god I had erected
> was a god of ideas
> that could be found in your head,
> dissected by your mind,
> and controlled and called upon when needed.
> I was worshiping dead branches
> that needed to be pruned away.

But over the years,
I was too stubborn to learn all at once
(I still am learning, just ask Wendy!)
the God who actively prowls about like midnight blazing fur
has eroded and broken down this false faith,
and by his power alone,
by his love alone,
has instilled in my heart
the desire,
the hunger,
the ravenous hunger,
to strive for a faith . . . for a life
that worships the LIVING GOD
and LIVES the greatest
foundation of the faith,
the grace,
the wondrous cleansing, soothing, peace-instilling grace,
of our Lord Jesus Christ,
the Love,
the profound, all powerful, all encompassing, passionate
Love of God,
and the Fellowship,
the binding, gathering, surrounding, clinging, grasping
Fellowship of the Holy Spirit.
The hope in that benediction we pastors often say
is really a hope for the deepest,
most intimate knowledge
of the very essence of God.

It is my hope and prayer for myself and for us all.

Blessings and Peace.
   Tom

Appendix A: The Survey

GOD EXPERIENCE SURVEY
Anonymous - just between you and God!
All responses will be aggregated as a whole;
no one will know your specific answers.
Please answer only those questions with which you feel comfortable.

Gender:

- Male
- Female

Age:

- 0-10
- 11-19
- 20-30
- 31-59
- 60-79
- 80+

I am: (check all that apply)

- ☐ Employed
- ☐ Homemaker
- ☐ Volunteer
- ☐ Retired
- ☐ Other

Name of Your Congregation:

Zip Code:

APPENDIX A: THE SURVEY

The Experience of God in Your Life

Overall in your life, how many days a week do you experience God's Presence?

- ○ One Day a Week
- ○ Two Days a Week
- ○ Three Days a Week
- ○ Four Days a Week
- ○ Five Days a Week
- ○ Six Days a Weeks
- ○ Seven Days a Week

Overall, when you experience God in your life it is …(1 hardly powerful, 5 extremely powerful)

	1	2	3	4	5
…How Powerful?	○	○	○	○	○

When I am in worship, I experience God …

	Hardly Ever	Some Sundays	Most Sundays	Every Time
How Often?	○	○	○	○

When I experience God in worship, it is ...(1 hardly powerful, 5 extremely powerful)

	1	2	3	4	5
...How Powerful?	○	○	○	○	○

During music, I experience God ...

	Hardly Ever	Sometimes	Most of the Time	Every Time
How Often?	○	○	○	○

When I experience God during the music, it is ...(1 hardly powerful, 5 extremely powerful)

	1	2	3	4	5
...How Powerful?	○	○	○	○	○

During the liturgy (for example: prayers, confession, Apostle's Creed, etc.), I experience God...

	Hardly Ever	Sometimes	Most of the Time	Every Time
How Often?	○	○	○	○

When I experience God during the liturgy, it is ... (1 hardly powerful, 5 extremely powerful)

	1	2	3	4	5
...How Powerful?	○	○	○	○	○

Service to the Church and the World

When I serve others, the community, or the church I experience God ...

	Hardly Ever	Sometimes	Most of the Time	Every Time
How Often?	○	○	○	○

When I experience God in service, it is ...(1 hardly powerful, 5 extremely powerful)

	1	2	3	4	5
...How Powerful?	○	○	○	○	○

Personal Time

When in nature, I experience God ...

	Hardly Ever	Sometimes	Most of the Time	Every Time
How Often?	○	○	○	○

When I experience God in nature, it is ...(1 hardly powerful, 5 extremely powerful)

	1	2	3	4	5
...How Powerful?	○	○	○	○	○

During times of hardship, how many days a week do you experience God?

- ○ One Day a Week
- ○ Two Days a Week
- ○ Three Days a Week
- ○ Four Days a Week
- ○ Five Days a Week
- ○ Six Days a Week
- ○ Seven Days a Week

When I experience God in times of hardship, it is ...(1 hardly powerful, 5 extremely powerful)

	1	2	3	4	5
...How Powerful?	○	○	○	○	○

APPENDIX A: THE SURVEY

For each of the next set of statements, please choose a number from 1 to 6. 1 = Very False; 6 = Very True.

Your Church

For each of the next set of statements, please choose a number from 1 to 6. 1 = Very False; 6 = Very True.

	1	2	3	4	5	6
1. People are willing to be vulnerable in my church	○	○	○	○	○	○
2. I have one or more good friends in my church	○	○	○	○	○	○
3. Our worship services are filled with hope and joy	○	○	○	○	○	○
4. I have studied the Bible extensively	○	○	○	○	○	○
5. Our church is very active in mission	○	○	○	○	○	○
6. Our church music is excellent and inspiring	○	○	○	○	○	○

APPENDIX A: THE SURVEY 149

7. I attend worship very regularly	○	○	○	○	○	○
8. Our worship space helps me feel the presence of God	○	○	○	○	○	○
9. I have an active, personal devotional life	○	○	○	○	○	○
10. My church is there for me in hard times.	○	○	○	○	○	○
11. I know my pastor very well. (For churches with more than one pastor, answer the question for the pastor you know the best)	○	○	○	○	○	○
12. My church should be more involved in justice.	○	○	○	○	○	○

13. I would attend more or be more involved in church if it more powerfully connected me to God's presence.   ○   ○   ○   ○   ○   ○

14. Church gets in the way of my experience of God.   ○   ○   ○   ○   ○   ○

15. Traditional worship is very important to me.   ○   ○   ○   ○   ○   ○

APPENDIX A: THE SURVEY 151

Personal Life: *Answer these next set of statements in regard to your own personal life.*

	1	2	3	4	5	6
1. I am conservative.	○	○	○	○	○	○
2. I give generously of my finances.	○	○	○	○	○	○
3. I am healthy.	○	○	○	○	○	○
4. I grew up going to church all the time.	○	○	○	○	○	○
5. I spend a lot of time outdoors.	○	○	○	○	○	○
6. I feel in my soul that God loves me.	○	○	○	○	○	○
7. God is powerfully active in the world.	○	○	○	○	○	○
8. I have someone in my life who loves me.	○	○	○	○	○	○
9. I experience God when I least expect it.	○	○	○	○	○	○
10. My family spends a lot of quality time together.	○	○	○	○	○	○

Daily Routine: *Work/Volunteer Life/homemaking: For these next set of questions, think about your daily routine. Whether it is homemaking, volunteering, employment, retirement activities, or something else. Answer these questions with that in mind.*

	1	2	3	4	5	6
1. My daily routine makes a difference in people's lives.	○	○	○	○	○	○
2. My daily routine uses my gifts.	○	○	○	○	○	○
3. At the end of day, I feel fulfilled.	○	○	○	○	○	○
4. I am appreciated for what I do.	○	○	○	○	○	○

Please share any thoughts you would like us to know about your experience of God.

_____
_____
_____
_____
_____

Please share one moment when you powerfully experienced the presence of God.

_____
_____
_____
_____
_____

If you would like to be contacted by your pastor, either about this survey or your faith journey, please write your name, email, and phone number here:

_____
_____
_____
_____

Appendix B: The Analysis

**Experiencing God –
Report of
First Presbyterian Church
Member Self-Rating Survey**

By: Dr. Thomas E. Evans
Dr. Jack R. Gallagher
Dr. John C. Lefebvre

October 10, 2019

God's Omnipresence

Background

Objectives

- **Design a survey methodology that can be used to assess:**
    - *Major ways in which Christians experience God*
    - *Extent to which Christians experience God*

- **Employee advanced statistical analytics to better understand God experiences by:**
    - Type of God Experience (**GE Type**)
    - Major predictors associated with experiencing God

- **Administer survey to members of First Presbyterian Church (FPC) of Spartanburg, SC**

- **Test and improve the survey methodology to render suitable for administration to other congregations**
    - Develop a database of responses that can be shared with other congregations wishing to administer it
    - Develop a methodology-description guide that can be shared with others

- **Present and discuss study findings and implications in various forums within FPC**

- **Share study methodology and current findings and implications with other congregations, church leaders and appropriate forums.**

APPENDIX B: THE ANALYSIS   157

Study Methodology

Types of God Experience – Study Framework

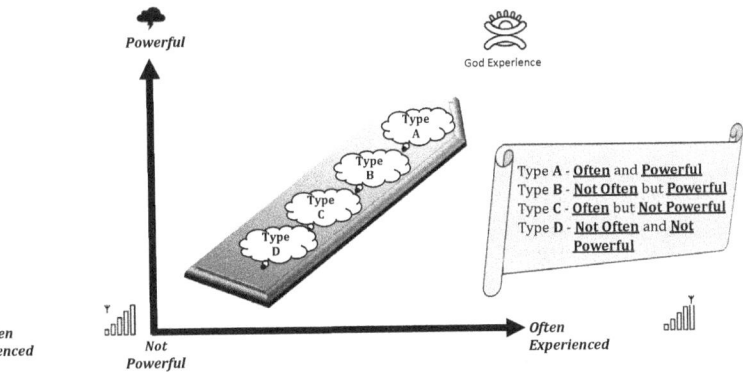

Type A - **Often** and **Powerful**
Type B - **Not Often** but **Powerful**
Type C - **Often** but **Not Powerful**
Type D - **Not Often** and **Not Powerful**

Four-Step Approach

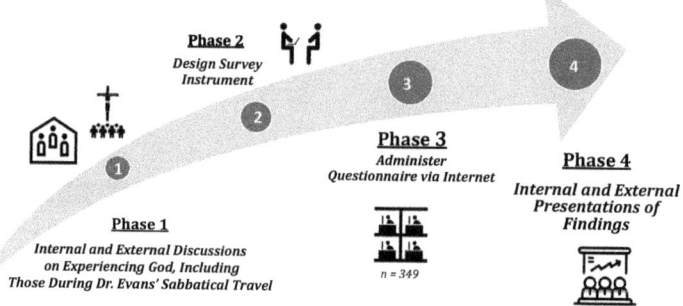

- **Phase 1**: Internal and External Discussions on Experiencing God, Including Those During Dr. Evans' Sabbatical Travel
- **Phase 2**: Design Survey Instrument
- **Phase 3**: Administer Questionnaire via Internet, n = 349
- **Phase 4**: Internal and External Presentations of Findings

Major Components of Survey Instrument

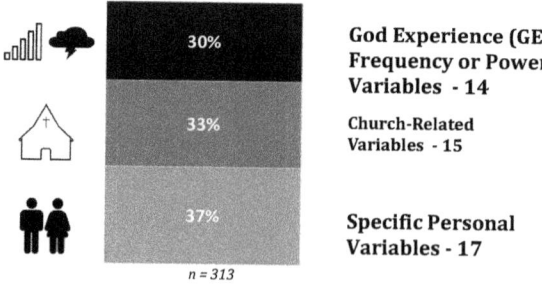

- 30% — God Experience (GE) Frequency or Power Variables - 14
- 33% — Church-Related Variables - 15
- 37% — Specific Personal Variables - 17

n = 313

Administered to congregation June 10-July 25, 2019

APPENDIX B: THE ANALYSIS   159

Rescaling Study Variables for Uniformity

Some questions had fewer response options than other, e.g.,

Q11 When I am in worship, I experience God ...
Hardly Ever (1)   Some Sundays (2)   Most Sundays (3)   Every Time (4)

How Often? (5)

Q24 When I experience God in times of hardship, it is ...
1 (1)   2 (2)   3 (3)   4 (4)   5 (5)

...How Powerful? (1)

Because scale uniformity is important for analysis and understanding, we rescaled all variables to 100 points.

For example for Q11, "1" became "25" - "2" became "50" .... "5" became "100"

for Q24, "1" became "20" - "2" became "40" .... "5" became "100."

Survey Statistical Power and Confidence Level

Statistical Power:

A percentage that tells you how much you can expect your survey results to reflect the views of the overall congregation if the sample is representative of it.

This survey has a minimum statistical power of 95% with a 95% confidence interval (p = 0.05) for all major variables compared.

Comparison of Survey Respondents and Total Congregation on Age and Gender

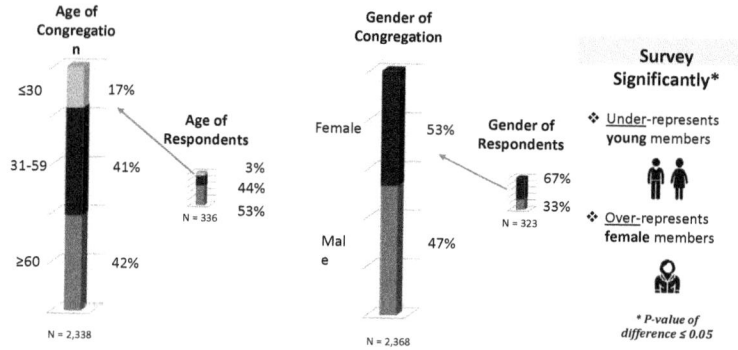

Analysis – Variable Correlations and Statistical Comparisons of High vs. Low Variable Ratings

Logistic regression analysis and **relative importance analysis**, described later, are **multivariate** analytical tools that allow us to consider **all** the **survey variables** simultaneously. However, there can be **great value** in analyzing and comparing **small sets** of study variable **combinations** of **special interest**.

The tables that resulted from analysis of the large number of **variable combinations** of interest are contained in **PDF files** located in the **Appendix**. Just click on a file for access.

- The 1st file includes:

- Correlation matrices that correlate each item in Section 1 (frequency and power of the experience of God) with each other item in section.
- The same matrices but correlating variables with variables in other sections combined.
- The 2nd file includes:

- Statistical (T-test) comparisons of the higher levels of responses in section 1 and if there is a difference between the higher and lower levels in terms of answers on other sections.

- The 3rd PDF file is the questionnaire.

APPENDIX B: THE ANALYSIS   161

Study Participant Characteristics

Primary Occupation of Survey Participants

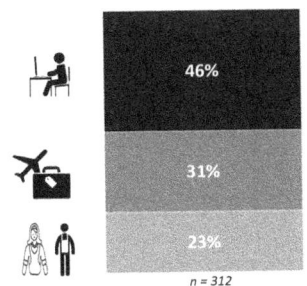

Employed — 46%
(Includes those who are employed pre-retirement and

Retired — 31%
(Includes those who are retired and also volunteer)

Homemaker — 23%
(Includes those who are homemakers and also volunteer)

n = 312
Distribution for total congregation not available

Proportion of Members by God Experience Type

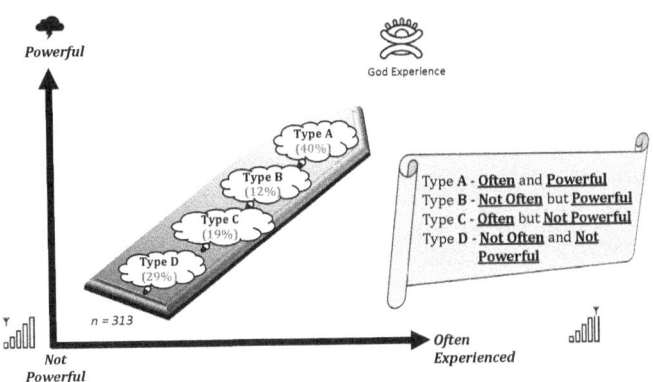

Type A - **Often** and **Powerful**
Type B - **Not Often** but **Powerful**
Type C - **Often** but **Not Powerful**
Type D - **Not Often** and **Not Powerful**

Type A (40%)
Type B (12%)
Type C (19%)
Type D (29%)

n = 313

Not Often Experienced / Often Experienced
Not Powerful / Powerful

APPENDIX B: THE ANALYSIS

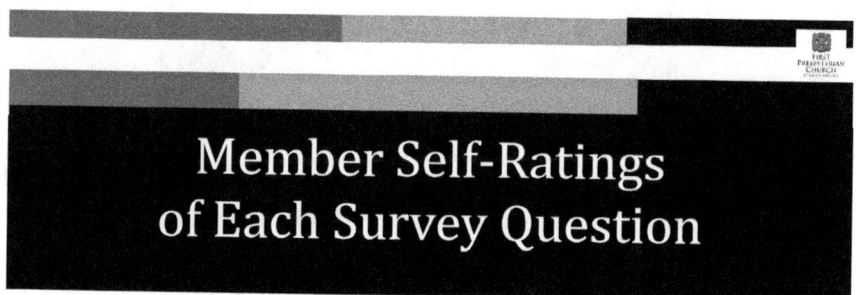

Mean Self-Rating of God Experience on Power and Frequency Variables

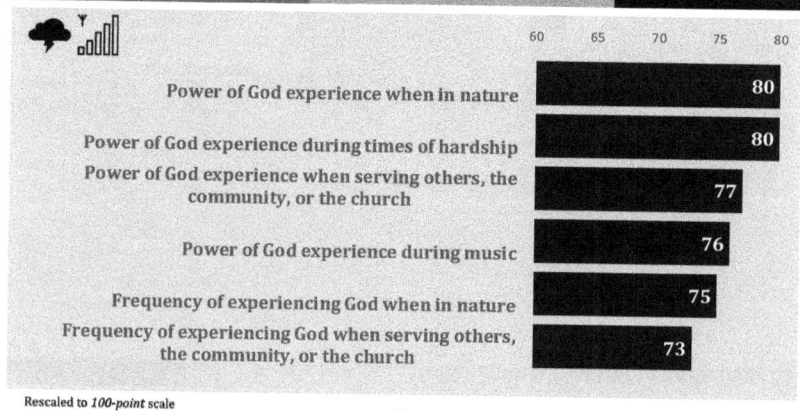

	Rating
Power of God experience when in nature	80
Power of God experience during times of hardship	80
Power of God experience when serving others, the community, or the church	77
Power of God experience during music	76
Frequency of experiencing God when in nature	75
Frequency of experiencing God when serving others, the community, or the church	73

Rescaled to *100-point* scale

APPENDIX B: THE ANALYSIS   163

Mean Self-Rating of God-Experience on Power and Frequency Variables *(continued)*

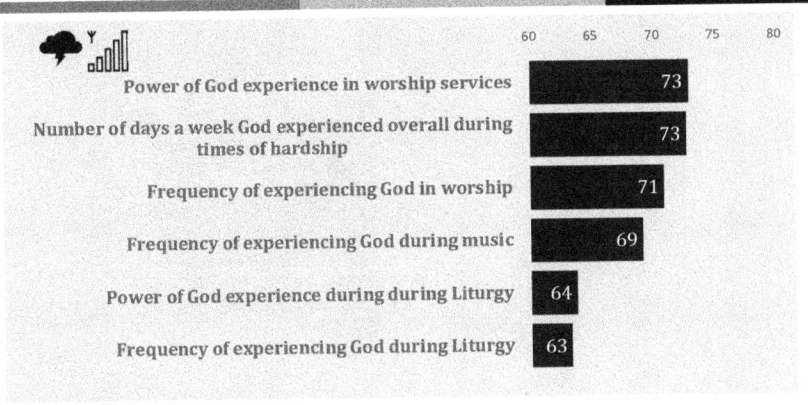

Rescaled to *100-point* scale

Mean Self-Rating of God-Experience on Church-Related Variables

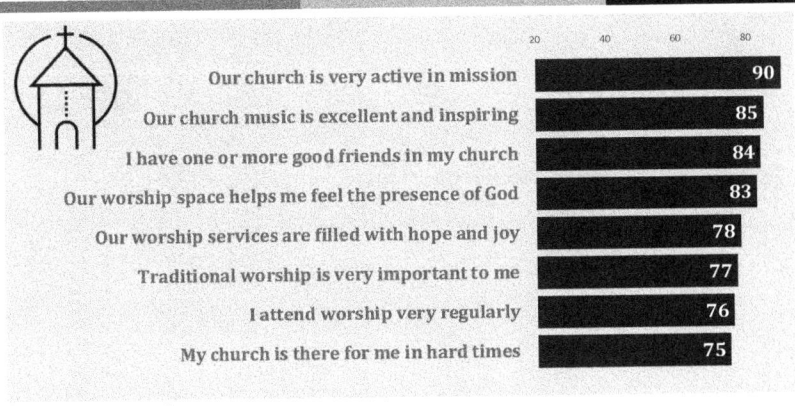

Rescaled to *100-point* scale

Mean Self-Rating of God-Experience on Church-Related Variables *(continued)*

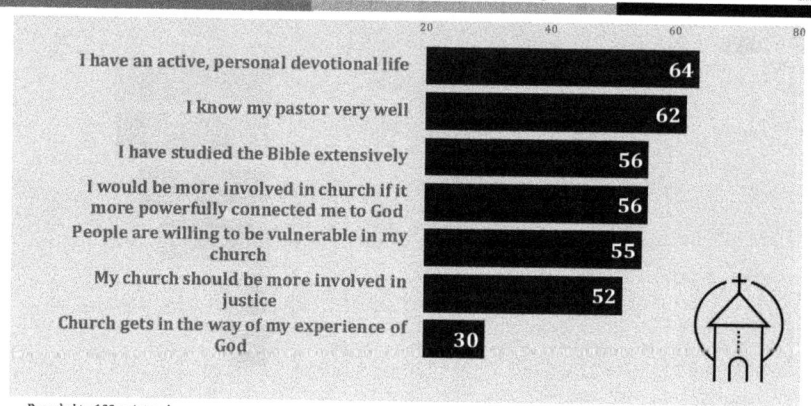

Variable	Rating
I have an active, personal devotional life	64
I know my pastor very well	62
I have studied the Bible extensively	56
I would be more involved in church if it more powerfully connected me to God	56
People are willing to be vulnerable in my church	55
My church should be more involved in justice	52
Church gets in the way of my experience of God	30

Rescaled to *100-point* scale

Mean Self-Ratings of God-Experience on Person-Specific Variables

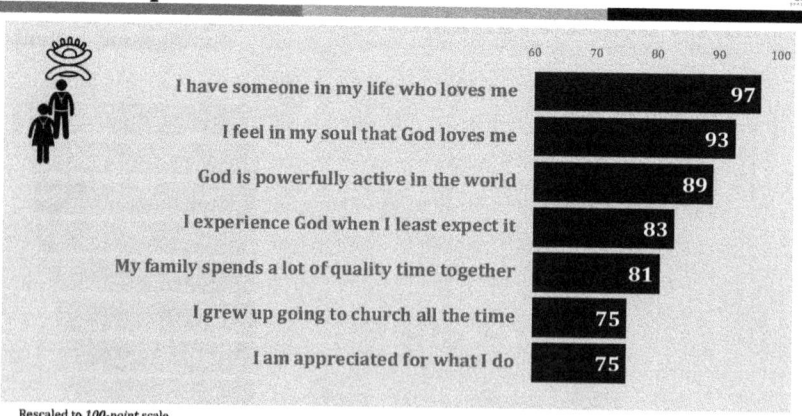

Variable	Rating
I have someone in my life who loves me	97
I feel in my soul that God loves me	93
God is powerfully active in the world	89
I experience God when I least expect it	83
My family spends a lot of quality time together	81
I grew up going to church all the time	75
I am appreciated for what I do	75

Rescaled to *100-point* scale

Mean Self-Ratings of God-Experience on Person-Specific Variables *(continued)*

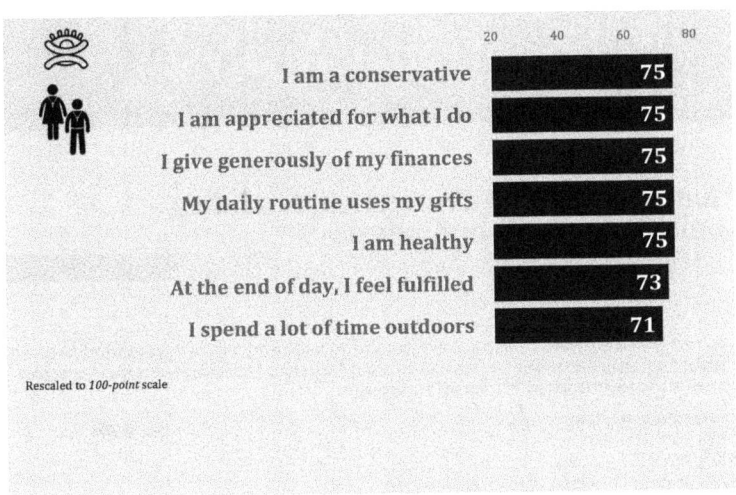

Rescaled to *100-point* scale

Regression & Relative Importance Analyses

Analysis: Advanced Analytical Modeling – Logistic Regression Analysis

Logistic regression analysis, a statistical tool, is a way of mathematically sorting out which of the study variables <u>accurately</u> predicts the outcome studied, e.g., which study variables predict the overall frequency and power of God experiences of FPC survey participants.

It answers these questions:
    Which tested factors matter most?
    Which merit less attention?
    How certain are we about all these factors?

Regression analysis:
    Explains a phenomenon that we want to understand
    Helps prioritize decision making.

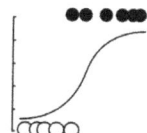

Of special note, it enables us to assess the individual (isolated) contribution of each significant predictor while **removing** the **confounding effects** of other tested factors (holding the other factors constant).

Often factors in regression analysis are associated but not connected by cause and effect.
    In some cases, follow-up research and discussion may help clarify this.

Supplementing Regression Analysis with Relative Importance Analysis, a New Explanatory Tool

Though **regression analysis** enables us to assess the individual (isolated) contribution of each significant predictor, it doesn't allow us to assess the <u>percentage</u> contribution of each predictor to the total prediction.

 We combined **traditional regression modeling** (logistic regression analysis with proportional odds) with a recently available[1] and powerful analytical methodology: **relative importance analysis (RIA)**, also known as **relative weights analysis (RWA)**.

This **combination of analytical tools** overcomes the pervasive and distorting problem in regression analysis of multicollinearity and provides a level of precision not possible otherwise.

Thus each model includes: **(1)** the **proportional odds** for each **significant individual predictor** when other **confounding tested factors** are **held constant** and **(2)** the **relative importance** of each of these variables (**percentage** each significant variable contributes to the total model prediction).

[1] First use of this combination methodology in the medical research literature was reported in this recent article: Gallagher, Jack R; Gudeman, Jennifer; Heap, Kylee; Vink, Joy; Carroll [Gallagher], Susan. Understanding If, How, and Why Women with Prior Spontaneous Preterm Births are Treated with Progestogens: A National Survey of Obstetrician Practice Patterns, **American Journal of Perinatal Reports (AJPR)**, 08(04):e315-e324, October 2018.

Model: Significant Predictors of Whether FPC Members Are God Experience (GE) Type A

- The dependent variable was derived from responses to the following questions:
    - *Overall in your life, how many days a week do you experience God's presence?*
      (options - from 1 to 7 days)
    - *Overall, when you experience God in your life it is how powerful?* *(5-point scale with "1" being "not at all powerful" and "5" being "Extremely Powerful")*

- **Data for the model extracted from 285 member questionnaires that contained no missing data** (a requirement for the analytical models used)

- The logistic regression model was statistically significant, $\chi2(7) = 358.289$, $p < .0005$. yielding an overall correct percentage of **76.4%**.

168 APPENDIX B: THE ANALYSIS

Predicting GE Type A Members from Logistic Regression and Relative Importance Modeling

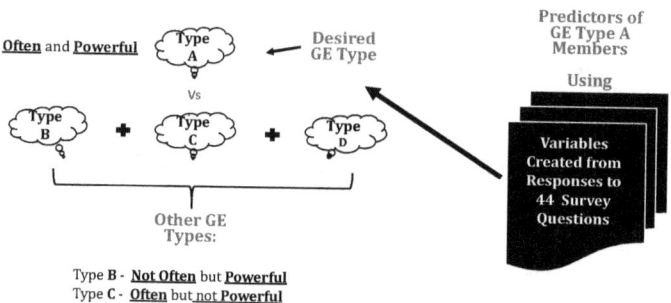

Type B - **Not Often** but **Powerful**
Type C - **Often** but **not Powerful**
Type D - **Not Often** and **Not Powerful**

When Other Tested Factors Are Held Constant:

1. A member who "experiences God most <u>frequently</u> during times of hardship" was 3% more likely to be a GE Type A than were other members for each additional point higher on the questionnaire scale. The <u>relative influence</u> of this factor on member likelihood of being Type A was **29%**.

2. A member who "experiences God most <u>powerfully</u> during times of hardship" was 3.6% more likely to be a GE Type A than were other members for each additional point higher on the questionnaire scale. The *relative influence* of this factor on member likelihood of being Type A was **23%**.

3. A member who "has an active, personal devotional life" was 1.3% more likely to be a GE Type A than other members for each additional point higher on the questionnaire scale; the <u>relative influence</u> of this factor on member likelihood of being Type A was **19%**.

4. A member who "experiences God most <u>frequently</u> by attending worship services" was 2.3% more likely to be a GE Type A than were other members for each additional point higher on the questionnaire scale. The relative influence of this factor on member likelihood of being Type A was **16%**.

5. A member who "experiences God most <u>powerfully</u> by attending worship services" was 2.7% more likely to be a GE Type A than were other members for each additional point higher on the questionnaire scale. The relative influence of this factor on member likelihood of being Type A was **13%**.

Five Major Predictors of Whether a Member's God Experiences Overall Are Frequent/Powerful

Predictors	p Value	Proportional Odds Ratio Exp (B)	Relative Influence (% of total)*
Member experiences God most frequently during times of hardship	<0.001	1.030	29%
Member experiences God most powerfully during times of hardship	0.002	1.036	23%
Member who has an active, personal devotional life	<0.001	1.013	19%
Member experiences God frequently by attending worship services	0.014	1.023	16%
Member experiences God powerfully by attending worship services	0.019	1.027	13%

* Confidence interval from top predictor to bottom: 18%-40%, 13%-33%, 9%-32%, 8%-24%, 6%-23%

Bibliography

Augustine of Hippo. *Confessions*. Overland Park: Digireads.com, 2015.
Book of Common Worship. Presbyterian Church (USA) Louisville: Westminster, 1993.
Calvin, John. *Calvin: Institutes of the Christian Religion*. Philadelphia: Westminster, 1960.
———. *Preface to the Genevan Psalter*. Grand Rapids: Christian Classics Ethereal Library. https://www.ccel.org/ccel/ccel/eee/files/calvinps.htm.
"Einstein Believed in a Theory of Spacetime That Can Help People Cope with Loss." Forbes, Dec. 28, 2016. https://www.forbes.com/sites/quora/2016/12/28/einstein-believed-in-a-theory-of-spacetime-that-can-help-people-cope-with-loss/#6c5d876555d2.
Guigo. *The Ladder of Monks: A Letter on Contemplative Life*. Kalamazoo: Cistercian, 1981.
Hugo, Victor. *The Man Who Laughs*. Boston: Little, Brown and Co., 1888.
Kenny, Charles. "2015: The Best Year in History for the Average Human Being." *The Atlantic*, Dec. 18, 2015. https://www.theatlantic.com/international/archive/2015/12/good-news-in-2015/421200/.
Luther, Martin. "Preface to the Babst Hymnal (1545)." In Luther's Works, edited by Ulrich S. Leupold, 53:333. Philadelphia: Fortress, 1965.
Maimonides. *Mishneh Torah: Laws of Oaths*. Translated by Eliyahu Touger. https://www.chabad.org/library/article_cdo/aid/973874/jewish/Shvuot-Chapter-12.htm.
Marty, Martin E. "Believers Babble over Bible." *Context: A Commentary on the Interaction of Religion and Culture* 33.15 (2001) n.p.
Merton, Thomas. *Letter to Dorothy Day: Catholic Voices in a World on Fire*. Morrisville: Lulu.com, 2005.
———. *No Man Is an Island*. New York: Mariner, 2002.
Oliver, Mary. *House of Light*. Boston: Beacon, 1992.
St. Therese of Lisieux. *The Story of a Soul: The Autobiography of the Little Flower*. Charlotte, NC: Tan, 2010.
Sutton, Ray. "The Bible and Anamnesis." *Forward in Christ*, Oct. 30, 2018. http://www.forwardinchristmagazine.com/2018/10/the-bible-and-anamnesis.html.
"The Theology and Place of Music in Worship." Reformed Church in America. https://www.faithward.org/the-theology-and-place-of-music-in-worship/.

www.ingramcontent.com/pod-product-compliance
Lightning Source LLC
Chambersburg PA
CBHW051100160426
43193CB00010B/1254